good things

good things

THE BEST OF MARTHA STEWART LIVING

Special thanks to the many stylists, art directors, photographers,
writers, and editors whose inspirational ideas for "good things" make up this volume.
Thanks also to the entire staff of MARTHA STEWART LIVING OMNIMEDIA and to everyone at
Oxmoor House, Clarkson Potter, Satellite Graphics, and Quebecor Printing whose
invaluable work helped produce this book.

The recipes and photographs in this work were previously published in MARTHA STEWART LIVING.

Manufactured in the United States of America
Library of Congress Catalog Number: 97-065957
ISBN: 0-8487-1628-0 (hardcover)
0-8487-1638-8 (paperback)

Art Director: Linda Kocur
Senior Editor: Bruce Shostak
Writer: Amy Conway

OVERLEAF, LEFT: A pear serves as a place card and napkin decoration; a name tag is tied to the stem with thin twine.
OVERLEAF, RIGHT: Miniature milk bottles hold just one or two stems apiece. Mass bottles together to form an impressive yet casual centerpiece. Set one at each place setting, or scatter them throughout the house.
OPPOSITE: Fresh cranberries anchor flower stems in a clear glass vase and add vibrant color to the arrangement.

contents

A few essentials, such as seed packets, gloves, and shears, make a perfect gift for a gardener, or party favors for an outdoor gathering. Pack them into terra-cotta pots, bundle with plain paper, and bind with green linen twine.

introduction

I have been using the phrase "It's a good thing" for as long as I can remember. When I started taping our television show almost five years ago, I thought it was very evocative to make the statement "It's a good thing" every time I did something neat, quick, particularly simple, or sensible. Those short projects, whether they involved cooking, gardening, or crafts, became an important part of MARTHA STEWART LIVING magazine as well, and a whole section of the front of our monthly publication was—and is—devoted to them.

Now everyone at MARTHA STEWART LIVING thinks the way I do when attempting to decide what is a "good thing" and what is not. The criteria for a "good thing" are complex, but straightforward. Is the project uncomplicated? Is it useful? Is it aesthetically pleasing? Is it something that many people will find interesting or pertinent to their lifestyle? Is it seasonal in nature? Are the materials used to complete the project easy to find? Is the result unusual?

This book brings together, for the first time, many of our best "good things." More than 200 are categorized by subject, and each is accompanied by clear, concise instructions, wonderful photographs, and oftentimes suggestions for using the ideas in creative and unusual ways. And we have provided the sources from which you can obtain many of the materials we used.

I am thrilled to think that the statement "It's a good thing" has actually resulted in this compendium of inexpensive and fun projects. I hope you enjoy these ideas as much as we at MARTHA STEWART LIVING have enjoyed creating them.

Martha Stewart

entertaining

The traditional etiquette of entertaining has evolved to include a few new rules: Relax, be creative, enjoy the planning and the party. Gatherings are guided by ease and simplicity; the atmosphere is comfortable and welcoming.

This chapter takes the decorative elements of entertaining—table settings, centerpieces, place cards—and shows you new ways to create them. Many of them fit smoothly into the more spontaneous, less formal gatherings that make sense for our busy lives. Whether you're having a cocktail party, an open house, or an intimate dinner, these ideas will assist and inspire you.

Follow them to the letter, or tailor them to your own style. Search your cupboards and find a new purpose for an old piece. Mix flea-market finds with your best china. Arrange handfuls of flowers in old glass tumblers, or fill a favorite bowl with fresh fruit and use it as a centerpiece. Often the perfect napkins or handmade place cards are all the adornment the table needs.

The setting can be elegant or whimsical, minimal or rich with texture and color. Let the occasion, the season, and your mood guide you. And have fun—that's the sure way to make certain your guests will, too.

Opposite: Antique decanters are often separated from their stoppers, but a miniature apple or pear can fill in for an evening. These diminutive fruits are available in the fall and winter, ideal for holiday entertaining. Top a flask of apple brandy with a tiny 'Winesap' or a lady apple, a flagon of Poire William with a 'Honeysweet' pear.

eggcup vases

Surprisingly versatile, eggcups can be used as both miniature vases and place cards. Use a matching set of eggcups, or put an eclectic collection to work. For the hydrangeas *(top left)* and the cluster of dried *Craspedia globosa* *(top center)*, cut the stems short and tie them with seam binding or ribbon; place the bouquet in an eggcup, allowing the seam binding to fall out of the cup. This technique can also be used with any fresh or dried flowers; for fresh ones, add a little water to the eggcup. The dried *Echinops* globe thistles *(top right)* are anchored in a 2-inch foam ball. Place the ball in the eggcup and trace around it with a pencil. Cut globe-thistle stems to ½ inch and poke them into the ball, using the circled surface as a guide. Lay a length of seam binding or ribbon into the eggcup with the ends over-hanging the edges and place the foam

natural settings

A napkin can do more than protect against crumbs and spills; it also provides a backdrop for a pretty flourish or a place card. The three stalks of wheat *(middle right)* are simply bound together with waxed linen wrapped in a tight coil. The wheat was found at a dried-flower shop; lavender or any delicate dried flower could be used instead. For the acorn tie *(bottom left)*, drill acorns through from cap to tip with a Dremel drill press. Thread an acorn onto each end of an 18-inch length of waxed linen thread; knot the ends to keep the acorns in place. Wrap the thread around a rolled napkin and tie on top. The herb initial *(bottom center)* is made

take your places

ball on top. For the name tags, cut out strips of art paper and punch a hole at one end. Fold them accordion-style, and write a name on each one, with one letter per square. Thread seam binding through the hole so the tag falls alongside the seam binding. Place one vase at each guest's setting.

from fresh thyme. A flexible thyme sprig is bent into the letter P; where the end of the sprig meets the stem of the letter, it is secured with thin twine. As the initial dries, it will keep its shape. Collect fallen leaves, like this oak leaf *(bottom right)*, and dry them flat for several days between the pages of a heavy book. Using a silver or gold paint pen, inscribe each guest's name on a leaf; place it over napkin.

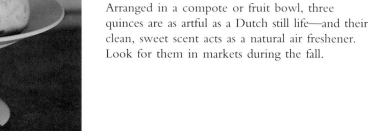

quince centerpiece

Quinces are most familiar in jars of jam, but here's a reason to bring them home fresh. Arranged in a compote or fruit bowl, three quinces are as artful as a Dutch still life—and their clean, sweet scent acts as a natural air freshener. Look for them in markets during the fall.

herb arrangement

In the late summer, herb gardens tend to overflow with more than is needed in any kitchen, so why not use the extra yield in a fragrant centerpiece? Mix shapes and textures, and add color with edible flowers and herb blossoms. This arrangement, which includes dill, rosemary, thyme, mint, basil, lavender, nasturtiums, and flowering herbs, sits in a high-sided bowl; a smaller bowl within keeps stems in place. A small pitcher, jar, or vase works just as well.

cuttings centerpiece

A centerpiece need not be restricted to what the name implies: a single arrangement in the table's center. Various leaves and cuttings that run the length of the table can form a dramatic decoration. Place each in its own bottle. Use houseplant trimmings, leaves from a florist, and cuttings from backyard ferns and shrubs; look for different sizes, textures, colors, and silhouettes.

plaid-and-striped linens

To make these cushions and the complementary tablecloth *(below and opposite)*, just choose a palette of two or three colors and look for fabric in varying—but not too busy—patterns.

To make the inner pillowcases fit snugly, like the ones on these 16-by-11-inch pillows, finished cases should be an inch smaller (15 by 10 inches).

1. For each one, cut fabric twice as wide as the finished case plus 4½ inches for overlap and hem allowance (34½ inches in this case), and as long as the finished case plus 1 inch. Hem each short end: Turn fabric ¼ inch, then 1¾ inches, then sew.

2. Fold short ends to center with right sides together so the hems overlap. Pin sides and sew with a ½-inch seam allowance.

3. Turn right side out; add buttonholes and buttons.

The outer coverings are new dish towels sewn into tubes the same dimensions as the pillows; attach 8-inch lengths of twill tape as ties.

To make a square tablecloth with a border: Choose the finished size you want, then choose the width of the finished border (this one is 10 inches). To determine the size of the center square, subtract twice the width of border, plus 1 inch for seam allowance, from dimensions of finished cloth. You will need four border strips; for each, the width should equal predetermined measurement (10 inches) plus 2 inches for hem and seam allowances; length should equal that of center square, plus twice the width of finished border, plus 3 inches for hem and seam allowances. Sew border strips to center square with a ½-inch seam allowance, stopping ½ inch from ends. Pin and stitch corners on the diagonal; trim excess fabric. Hem all the way around (½ inch, then 1 inch), and press flat.

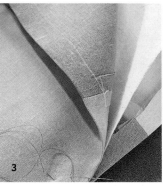

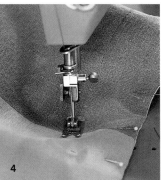

linen table mat

A table-size mat combines the elegance of a tablecloth with the convenience of a place mat. Made from eight linen panels in complementary colors (four on each side), it can be reversed according to the season; a layer of cotton flannel between the front and back adds heft and substance.

Before cutting and sewing, wash (or dry-clean) all fabrics to allow for shrinkage, and press flat.

To determine the size of the finished mat, measure your tabletop and subtract an inch from the length and width—the mat should be just a bit smaller than the table. Cut a piece of cotton flannel to those dimensions. Fold the flannel in quarters. Measure one of the quarters and add ⅜ inch to each side; this new measurement is the size of each linen block. Cut eight pieces of linen to this size.

1. Pin two linen blocks together, and sew with a ⅜-inch seam allowance; press seams open. Repeat, making four pairs of blocks.
2. Pin and sew two pairs together to complete one side of the mat; press seams open. Repeat with the other two pairs.
3. Fold a ⅜-inch hem all the way around the edge of both panels; press flat. Lay the flannel pad between the two panels and pin ½ inch from edges to secure. Sew the front and back together using an invisible stitch, securing the flannel between the panels; adjust the edges as you go to keep them even.
4. On the sewing machine, sew all the way around 2 inches from the edges.
5. This topstitching stabilizes the layers and gives the mat a crisp finish.

setting an outdoor table

A few clever accessories make setting a summer table as simple as it should be. A mat made from a matchstick window blind isn't likely to blow away in a breeze, and oversize terry-cloth napkins are ideal for mopping messy hands after a barbecue. Remove any hardware from the blind, and cut it to desired length. Turn under ½ inch of each side along which the sticks run lengthwise; secure this hem with wood glue. With a small saw, cut two pieces of ¾-inch-thick bamboo (available in garden centers) to the width of the blind; tie one piece to each hemmed end using waxed cotton cord or other thin, sturdy string *(top right)*. For the napkins *(above right)*, use terry cloth that is looped on both sides. Cut it into 20- to 24-inch squares. Pin seam binding all around the edge of each square, folding the seam binding at the corners so it lies flat; sew into place. After the meal, throw the napkins into the wash, shake crumbs out of the mat, and roll it up until the next time you dine outdoors.

ivy tablecloth

Ivy is a symbol for fidelity, so it's a fitting decoration for weddings—but this idea is also appropriate for any celebration, indoors or out. Begin with an inexpensive sheer tablecloth, or make one by hemming a square of organza or tulle. Cut equal-size ivy leaves, with their stems attached, from the vines. Hot-glue the leaves to the border of the cloth in a zigzag pattern, tucking each stem under the preceding leaf. The leaves will stay fresh for a few days. After the party, remove the leaves; the dried glue should unstick easily from the tablecloth.

embossed napkins

Here's one way to make your mark: Emboss initials onto plain paper napkins when you're entertaining a crowd. Embossers can be found at some stationery stores and rubber-stamp companies; for a custom monogram, browse through books of typography, and have the embosser cast to order.

making napkins

Finding napkins in the color, size, and style you want shouldn't be difficult—but it is. When you make your own, you get exactly what you want, whether it's linen with a box corner or cotton with polka dots. Instructions for these eight napkins are given on the following pages, and you can also modify them to come up with new designs. Experiment with different fabrics, such as men's shirting or organdy, but stick to natural fibers for their absorbency—even the prettiest napkin has to be practical.

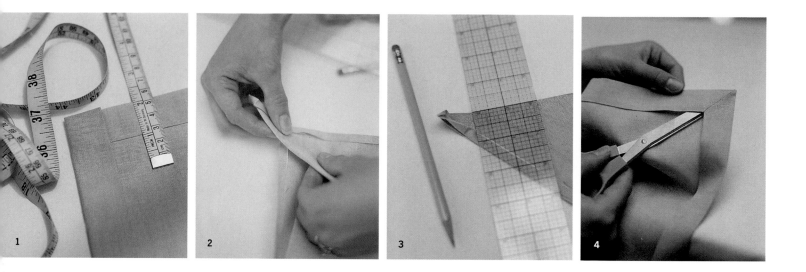

mitering corners

To make a 24-inch-square napkin, start with a 26½-inch square of fabric (this is pinpoint-oxford-cloth cotton).

1. Turn and press all edges under ¼ inch, then again 1 inch.

2. At one corner, open out the 1-inch hem on both sides and fold the napkin back on itself on the diagonal, with right sides together.

3. Lay the fold flat on a work surface. Lay a ruler across the corner perpendicular to the diagonal fold, starting where the 1-inch crease meets the fold. Draw a pencil line, and stitch along it. Trim the corner to ¼ inch from seam. Press seam open.

4. Turn corner right side out, following 1-inch creases. Press. Repeat with remaining corners. To finish, stitch hem down, all the way around.

contrast facing

To make a 25-inch-square napkin, cut two 25½-inch squares of handkerchief linen in contrasting colors. Pin together with right sides facing. Stitch ¼ inch from edges all around, leaving a 3-inch opening. Trim corners, turn right side out, and press. Finish by stitching ⅟₁₆ inch from edge (left) to close gap.

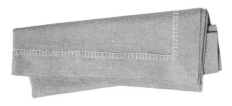

blanket stitching

Start by making a mitered-corner napkin (see opposite page); instead of machine-stitching the hem, use a decorative blanket stitch. Work on the napkin's wrong side, from left to right. With five-strand embroidery thread, make the first stitch down through the hem and fabric ¼ inch in from hem edge at one corner; leave a 2-inch tail of thread free to tuck inside the hem. Bring needle up through fabric just above hem edge, opposite the first stitch; pull through. Make a second stitch into the hem ¼ inch to the right of the first; when you draw the needle up through the fabric, keep the loose thread behind the needle. As the stitch is pulled tight, the thread will form an L. Continue stitching all the way around. Finish with a knot and tuck a 2-inch tail of thread inside the hem.

embroidering dots

Start with a napkin 24 inches square. Make a same-size pattern of tissue paper; use a ruler to mark it with a 2-inch grid. Mark a dot at every other intersection running horizontally and vertically—there should be sixty-one dots. Lay pattern over the napkin and pin through dot centers into fabric. Remove pattern. From fusible interfacing, cut out sixty-one ½-inch circles. Place each circle where a pin falls. Iron to fuse. Stitch over each dot with embroidery thread, working by machine or by hand.

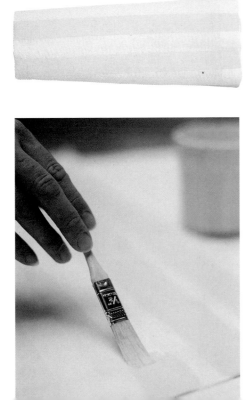

painting stripes

Start with a cotton or linen napkin of any size. Wash to remove sizing, and press. Using a pencil and ruler, mark 1-inch intervals along one side. Block off alternating stripes with 1-inch-wide masking tape. Apply fabric paint onto the exposed fabric, creating stripes. Let dry for about thirty minutes; remove tape. To set the design, heat iron to medium and iron painted napkin facedown on scrap fabric for two minutes.

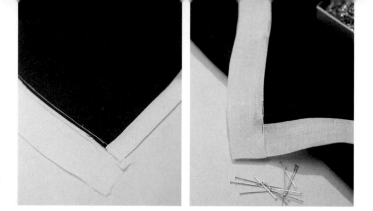

contrasting hems

To make a 24-inch-square napkin, cut a 23¼-inch square of handkerchief linen. You will also need four strips of fabric for the hem, each 3 by 26 inches.

1. Fold one long edge of each strip under ¼ inch; press.

2. Lay one strip over fabric so strip's unpressed edge lines up with one fabric edge (strip's ends will extend past the ends of the fabric square). Pin and stitch with a ¼-inch seam.

3. Trim darker fabric to ⅛ inch. Press strip out flat, as shown *(top left)*. Fold strip over seam allowance to other side of fabric square, enclosing stitching. Pin and press.

4. Stitch strip to square 1⁄16 inch in from turned edge. Trim ends to meet ends of square.

5. Repeat, attaching another strip on adjacent side, but before folding strip over, turn under and press end of strip at corner formed with hemmed strip to align with hemmed edge; pin *(top right)*. Stitch around corner to make a box, then stitch down second hemmed side. Repeat, hemming remaining sides.

self-striping

To make a 25-inch-square napkin, cut five rectangles from two different colors of handkerchief linen, three of one color, two of another. Each rectangle should be 5½ by 25½ inches. Stitch strips together, alternating colors, along long sides with a ¼-inch seam. Press seams flat to run in same direction. Continue as directed for the contrast-faced napkin (see page 22), using the resulting square as one of the two sides.

box corners

To make a 32-inch-square napkin, cut a 36½-inch square of fabric, such as this cotton organdy. Turn and press one edge under ¼ inch, then 2 inches; pin in place. Repeat on the clockwise adjacent edge, so the second turned side encloses the corner of the first. Repeat, folding and pinning all four edges. The box corners should be 2 inches square. Stitch hem to fabric 1⁄16 inch from hem edge by sewing down one side, through box corner to napkin edge; pivot and stitch around box. Stitch along the next side and around box as before; continue until entire hem is sewn.

monogramming napkins

A monogram is all it takes to turn an ordinary dish towel into a civilized oversize napkin. Look for vintage linens at flea markets, or use new towels. To embroider the initial by hand, find a type-style you like by looking through books of typography, or draw a letter yourself. Transfer the letter to the fabric by tracing over it with sewing transfer paper. For block letters, use cross-stitches; for curvier, more fluid letters, use French knots or satin stitches. You can also bring the towels to a monogrammer, who will do the stitching.

quick place cards

Some of the easiest, most festive place cards use natural materials that are in season. Here, a sweet-gum-tree spur has a name tag tied to its stem. For other ideas, just look around; inspiration is everywhere. Try tagging the following items: small gourds and pumpkins, pears and apples, a sprig of holly, pinecones, seashells, miniature ears of Indian corn, a bundle of cinnamon sticks, fresh or dried flowers, baby eggplants and pattypan squashes, or cacti in little terra-cotta pots. Use stiff paper for the name tags, and tie them on with thin ribbon or cord in a color that complements the rest of the table setting.

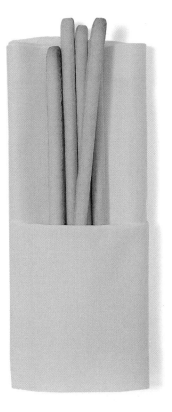

napkin ties

With these decorations, unfolding a napkin is like unwrapping a little package, making any meal feel like a celebration. A cellophane bag of pumpkin seeds *(top left)* is cinched with waxed linen thread and decorated with an oak leaf cut from colored paper. To make a pocket for breadsticks *(top center)*, fold top and bottom edges of a napkin to the center; fold bottom up again to cover the edges, then fold two sides to the back. A glassine envelope with two crescent cookies *(top right)* is tied around a napkin. A rolled-up napkin *(bottom left)* is encircled by a sprig of flowering oregano; a 6-inch length of florist's wire is bound to its stem with floral tape. The pinecone *(bottom right)* has an eye screw twisted into its top; elegant ribbon is laced through the eye and tied around the napkin.

pitcher cover

Sweet summer drinks are as appealing to bugs as they are to people. Keep insects out of pitchers and jugs with a weighted fabric cover. Here, vintage Bakelite zipper pulls hang from the corners of a pretty handkerchief; buttons and beads could be stitched around the edge of a cloth instead.

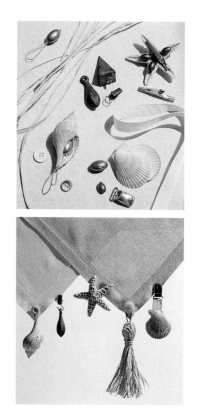

button napkin rings

These napkin rings give you a good reason to raid the button box. Cut 1¼-inch elastic into 6-inch lengths; hand-stitch ends together. Sew on buttons, overlapping them, to cover elastic completely. These are made with vintage Bakelite buttons, which can be found at flea markets and antiques stores, but any colorful, plastic buttons would work just as well.

tablecloth weights

Breezes make outdoor dining more pleasant, until the tablecloth sails. Lead weights will keep everything in place. *Above, from left:* **tulip-shell weight**—Loop a piece of cord, knot the ends, and pass loop through a lead bead. Glue bead to hollow of shell, and bring cord through the shell's open tip. Hang from a button.
lead fishing weight—This one is simply fastened to a curtain-clip hook.
starfish weight—Glue a lead bead and electrical clip to underside of a starfish.
raffia tassel weight—Pass a loop of raffia through a lead bead; wrap lengths of raffia over bead and tie in a bundle. Hang from a button sewn to cloth.
scallop-shell weight—Glue a lead-weight bead inside half a scallop shell. Thread ribbon through a suspender clip, glue into other half of shell, and glue halves together.

basket liners

Linen-lined baskets are used in Europe to hold rising bread dough, but they're practical for serving bread, too. Measure the inside dimensions of basket, both sides and bottom. Add two inches all around; cut unbleached linen to that size. With heavy thread and a sturdy needle, sew fabric into basket along inside bottom edge. Pleat cloth to fit sides or corners; secure each pleat with one stitch the depth of the basket. Finish by folding under and stitching linen around outside lip.

ice bowls

To make these elegant ice sculptures, you don't need a chisel or a blow torch. You will need two glass or stainless-steel bowls; one should fit inside the other with ½ to 1 inch of space between them. Scatter edible flowers, herbs, or citrus slices in the large bowl and place the smaller bowl inside. Tape so tops of bowls are flush. Pour water between bowls to ½ inch from top; add more flowers and arrange them with a skewer. Freeze overnight. To unmold, let bowls stand at room temperature on a dish towel for 10 to 20 minutes; do not run under water. Untape, lift out top bowl, and invert ice bowl out of mold. Freeze until ready to use. Experiment with different uses and shapes: A bowl with dill sprigs can hold boiled shrimp; floral bowls are good for ice cream or sorbet. The fluted bowl was made using two brioche molds.

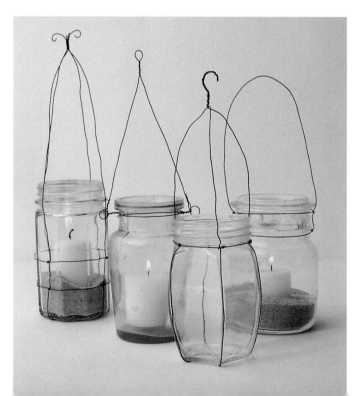

candlelight reflectors

When candles were the only source of light after sunset, reflective backdrops were used to intensify the flame's glow. With these old-fashioned holders, nickel silver deepens the glow of candlelight while a pastry tin catches any drips.

1. Measure the height and width of a pillar candle. On a sheet of 26-gauge nickel silver, use a grease pencil to draw a rectangle that is 1 inch wider and up to 7 inches longer than the candle. Draw a bend-line 4 inches up from the bottom; draw a curved outline to finish the ends, or taper the sides.

2. Wearing protective gloves, use metal snips to cut along the outlines. File rough edges with a metal file. Bend at the bend-line.

3. Before decorating the edges, cover a work surface with scrap wood. For a fluted edge, hammer a flat-head screwdriver at ⅛-inch intervals into the metal. For holes, hammer a center punch through the metal at ⅛-inch intervals. On the base, rest a tart tin to hold a candle.

hanging jar lanterns

Enjoy candlelight outdoors with hanging hurricane lanterns, which protect flames from the evening breeze. They are made from heat-proof glass jars and 20-gauge annealed iron wire. To cut and bend wire, you'll need wire cutters and pliers; jeweler's tools work well. If the jar has a thick lip, the handle can be attached just below the lip; otherwise, fashion a cage to support the jar. Strength is the foremost consideration in the handle's design, but the handle can be whimsical or plain. Before hanging, fill each jar partway with sand to anchor the votive candle, keeping it from toppling if the lantern sways.

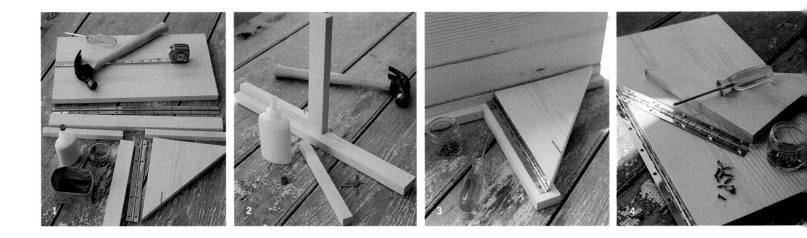

folding shelf

For summertime entertaining, the cooking is done on the grill—but there are never enough countertops nearby. This folding shelf, attached to a wall near the eating area or grill, provides extra space for plates, food, and barbecue tools.

1. You'll need the following supplies, available at hardware stores and lumberyards: two stainless-steel piano hinges, one 18 inches long, the other 9 inches; eight 1¼-inch finishing nails; twenty-eight ½-inch stainless-steel screws; carpenter's glue. You'll also need six pieces of ¾-inch-thick pine planking cut to these measurements: an 18-by-10-inch rectangle; a length 18 by 1½ inches; two lengths 8¼ by ¾ inches; a length 9½ by 1½ inches; and a right-angled triangle measuring 8 by 9 by 12 inches. Seal each piece with shellac or weatherproof paint.

2. Position the 9½-inch length of planking upright on the midpoint of the 18-inch length and flush with one edge, as shown. Glue and nail together, making a T shape. Lay the two 8¼-inch lengths on top of the 18-inch length, also flush with the edge. Glue and nail in place.

3. Screw one side of the 18-inch piano hinge to one of the long edges of the 18-by-10-inch rectangle. Attach one side of the 9-inch hinge to the 9-inch edge of the triangle.

4. Lay the T shape flat. Screw the unattached side of the triangle's 9-inch hinge to the 9½-inch length of the T shape, down the center and flush with the 18-inch length. Finally, attach the 18-inch rectangle—the shelf itself—to the T by screwing the unattached side of its hinge to the edge of the 18-inch length; make sure the shelf hinges downward.

Attach the collapsible shelf to an outdoor wall using the appropriate fasteners: masonry anchors for brick, wood screws for wood. It will hang unobtrusively until dinnertime.

cooking

Some of the best things from the kitchen are also the easiest. In this chapter you will find chef's secrets, tips, and tricks, as well as homemade treats, all of them ingenious in their simplicity.

In the kitchen, success begins with the freshest, best-quality ingredients. They scarcely need embellishment. A perfectly ripe piece of fruit is a ready-made dessert. A tomato that falls from the vine into your hand needs only a sprinkling of salt. Enjoy favorite foods again and again while they are plentiful, then wait out the months until their season returns. Indulge in wonderful olive oil and the best baking chocolate; you will taste the difference.

But cooking is always easier with the proper methods. A series of tips teaches basic techniques and a few unusual ones. They will transform the way you work in the kitchen. Try them once, and you won't forget them.

And keep in mind that the most inspired recipe will not necessarily be the most complicated and difficult one. It takes every bit as much confidence to prepare the simplest food, which may just be the most appreciated of all.

Opposite: Thousands of years ago, the mustard plant was discovered as a food flavoring. Its seeds range in color and intensity from the mildest yellow or white to hot brown to powerful, pungent black. These homemade blends balance hot, sweet, spicy, and mild flavors. Packaged as acorns, they also make perfect presents.

ABOVE LEFT AND RIGHT: Homemade mustards, made by blending an array of seeds and spices, are easily packaged as gifts. RIGHT: Flavored oils are ideal for drizzling over grilled fish or meats. BELOW: In these syrups, berries and orchard fruits provide the perfect counterpart to maple's mellow sweetness.

blackberry blueberry maple syrup

strawberry nectarine maple syrup

pear vanilla maple syrup

raspberry blackberry maple syrup

apricot maple syrup

homemade mustards

To decorate the jars, pull a double layer of tissue down over the lid, and secure with a rubber band. Bring tissue back up, cinch with twine, and trim with scissors.

EACH MAKES ABOUT 3 CUPS

English Mustard

    1 cup brown mustard seeds
    ¼ cup yellow mustard seeds
    1 cup dark beer
    1¼ cups white-wine vinegar
    1 cup mustard powder combined
        with 1 cup water (let sit 20 minutes)
    1 teaspoon sugar
    1 teaspoon salt
    1 teaspoon ground allspice
    ¼ teaspoon ground turmeric
    ¼ teaspoon ground mace

Red-Wine Mustard

    ⅔ cup yellow mustard seeds
    ½ cup brown mustard seeds
    1 cup red-wine vinegar
    ½ cup dry red wine
    1 teaspoon freshly ground pepper
    2 tablespoons sugar
    2 teaspoons salt
    1 tablespoon dried marjoram

Green-Peppercorn Mustard

    ½ cup yellow mustard seeds
    ¼ cup black mustard seeds
    ¾ cup balsamic vinegar
    ½ cup dry sherry
    2 tablespoons green peppercorns
    ⅓ cup olive oil
    2 teaspoons salt

Pink-Peppercorn Mustard

    Same ingredients as Green-Peppercorn
    Mustard, but substitute 2 tablespoons pink
    peppercorns for green, white-wine vinegar
    for balsamic, and add 3 tablespoons
    chopped fresh tarragon

1. In a nonreactive container, combine mustard seeds with alcohol (if called for) and vinegar. Let sit 48 hours. Check periodically to make sure seeds are covered by liquid; add more if necessary.
2. Combine seed mixture and remaining ingredients in a food processor. Process until creamy, 4 to 6 minutes.

3. Pack into clean glass jars, and refrigerate for three to four weeks for flavors to come together before using.

flavored oils

These simple sauces are intensely flavored and remarkably versatile. In the grapefruit oil, you can try orange juice instead. In the cilantro oil, substitute basil, parsley, or mint; vary the amount of herbs to make as much or as little of this oil as you like.

Pink-Grapefruit-and-Cilantro Oil

    2 cups fresh pink-grapefruit juice, strained
    ¼ cup Cilantro Oil (see below) or canola oil

In a saucepan over medium heat, reduce the juice to a thin syrup, about ¼ cup. Combine with oil in a glass jar. Cover and shake well. Refrigerate for up to two weeks. Shake before using.
MAKES ¼ CUP

Cilantro Oil

    1 large bunch cilantro
    Extra-virgin olive oil

1. Blanch cilantro leaves and some stems. Refresh in cold water; pat dry.
2. Purée leaves in a blender with an equal amount of oil. Pour into a glass jar and add twice as much oil as purée mixture. Cover and shake well.
3. Refrigerate mixture overnight. Bring to room temperature, and pour through a strainer lined with damp cheesecloth. Do not press on the solids. Refrigerate oil, covered, for up to two weeks.

Spice Oil

    2 tablespoons ground spice, such as chile
        or curry powder
    1 cup canola oil

1. Mix the spice with a little water to make a smooth paste. Place in a glass jar, and add oil. Shake well, and let sit, unrefrigerated, for two days.

2. Carefully pour oil through a strainer lined with damp cheesecloth. Stored at room temperature, oil will keep for several months.
MAKES 1 CUP

Bell-Pepper Oil

    4 to 5 red or yellow bell peppers
    Extra-virgin olive oil

1. Put peppers through a juice extractor; they should yield about 1 cup of juice. In a small saucepan over low heat, reduce by half; strain. Pour into a clean saucepan, and reduce to a syrup; there will be about ¼ cup.
2. Pour syrup into a small glass jar and add an equal amount of oil. Cover and shake well; store in the refrigerator for up to two weeks. Shake before using.
MAKES ½ CUP

fruit syrups

Use pretty glass bottles if you're giving the syrup as a gift. Tie on a handwritten tag with thin ribbon or waxed twine. To flavor the syrups, use a mix of several fruits or just one kind.

MAKES 3 CUPS

    2 cups berries or diced fruit (pitted or
        cored), such as pears, peaches, or plums
    1 cup maple syrup
    1 vanilla bean (optional)

1. Combine fruit and syrup in a small bowl. If using berries, press them with the back of a spoon until they just start to break apart. For a smoother syrup, press through a sieve.
2. Split vanilla bean, if using, and scrape seeds into mixture. Add bean to bowl.
3. Transfer mixture to a clean bottle or container, cover, and refrigerate. Use within three or four days. Before serving, the syrup can be warmed in a small saucepan over low heat.

LEFT AND ABOVE: Low-fat vegetable crisps.
RIGHT AND ABOVE RIGHT: Easy fritatta hors
d'oeuvres. BELOW AND BELOW RIGHT: Making
potato, sweet-potato, and onion latkes.

low-fat vegetable crisps

Dried in the microwave, these vegetables are addictive—yet they have little or no fat. Microwave ovens with carousels dry more evenly; watch ingredients carefully if drying in a microwave without one.

    Carrots, peeled and trimmed
    Potatoes (all varieties, including sweet
      potatoes), washed, not peeled
    Turnips, trimmed, not peeled
    Celery root, peeled
    Leeks, washed and trimmed to 5 inches
    Seasonings, such as coarse salt, cayenne,
      cumin, paprika, and wasabi powder
    Bell peppers, sliced into thin strips
    Raw, unsalted pumpkin seeds (available in
      health-food stores; also called pepitas)
    Canned chickpeas, rinsed and drained
    Frozen green peas, thawed
    Fresh sage and rosemary leaves
    Chives
    Sprouts, such as mung bean, lentil, mixed
      crunchy, and wheat

1. On a mandoline, slice carrots, potatoes, and turnips paper-thin lengthwise or widthwise; slice celery root and leeks lengthwise. Rerinse leeks.

2. Arrange one kind of vegetable in a single layer on a double layer of paper towel. Sprinkle with seasoning if desired.

3. Microwave on high; the following are approximate times. Carrots and bell peppers: 2 minutes, turn, 2 minutes more. Sweet potatoes, turnips, celery: 2 minutes, turn, 1½ minutes more. Potatoes: 1½ minutes, turn, 1½ minutes more. Leeks: 1½ minutes, turn, 1 minute more. Pumpkin seeds: 8 to 9 minutes, turning every 3 minutes. Chickpeas and green peas: 8 to 10 minutes, turning every 3 minutes. Sage, rosemary, chives: 1 minute, turn, 1 minute more. Sprouts: 6 to 8 minutes, turning every 3 minutes. When done, the vegetables will feel dry to the touch.

4. Let cool. Store in airtight containers up to three days; keep green peas in an open container and eat within two days.

potato, sweet-potato, and onion latkes

Serve this version of classic Hanukkah latkes at any cocktail party. In the two variations, unexpected ingredients provide a delicious contrast to the potatoes.

MAKES 2 DOZEN 2-INCH LATKES

    1 all-purpose or Yukon gold potato (about
      10 ounces)
    1 sweet potato (about 10 ounces), peeled
    ¼ large white onion, peeled
    1 large egg at room temperature
    2 tablespoons all-purpose flour
    1 teaspoon salt, or more to taste
    ¼ teaspoon freshly ground pepper
      Vegetable oil, for frying

1. Grate potatoes and onion using the largest holes of a four-sided grater. Place in a small bowl, and add the egg, flour, salt, and pepper; stir well to combine.

2. Heat 1 tablespoon oil in a large non-stick skillet over medium-high heat. Drop heaping tablespoonfuls of batter into the pan, and cook until golden brown around the edges, about 3 minutes. Turn latkes over, press lightly with a spatula, and cook about 3 minutes more. Continue cooking latkes in batches until batter is used up.

3. Serve with applesauce or sour cream.

Potato, Carrot, and Parsnip Latkes:

Use 2 all-purpose potatoes, 1 medium carrot, and 1 small parsnip.

Potato, Onion, and Horseradish Latkes:

Use 2 Yukon Gold potatoes, ¼ large white onion, and 2 tablespoons prepared horseradish, liquid pressed out.

easy hors d'oeuvres

Hors d'oeuvres for a crowd are the home-made equivalent of fast food when you make them in mini-muffin tins. Try these little frittatas or your own favorite recipes for corn bread, quiche, or sweet or savory muffins. Don't forget to chop fillings extra-fine, and bake for about a third as long as you normally would—eight to ten minutes for most recipes.

MAKES 48

    1 medium zucchini
    4 to 6 white mushrooms
    1 red bell pepper
    1 yellow bell pepper
    16 large eggs
    2 teaspoons salt
    ¾ teaspoon freshly ground pepper
    1 tablespoon chopped chives
    ½ cup finely grated Gruyère or fontina
      cheese
      Vegetable-oil cooking spray

1. Lightly spray two 24-mini-muffin tins with vegetable-oil spray. Slice the zucchini into ⅛-inch rounds. Slice the mushrooms lengthwise into ⅛-inch pieces. Core and seed the red and yellow bell peppers. Chop into ⅛-inch dice, and set aside.

2. Heat oven to 400°. In a large mixing bowl, whisk together the eggs, salt, pepper, and chives, and set aside. Arrange the cut zucchini, mushrooms, and peppers in each muffin tin. Ladle egg mixture into each tin, just even with the rim, and sprinkle with cheese.

3. Transfer to the oven and bake until frittatas are set, 8 to 10 minutes. Serve warm or reheat briefly at 325°.

LEFT: The best hot chocolate needs only pure chocolate, scalded milk, and, if you wish, mint or vanilla. ABOVE: Smooth and rich homemade fruit butters are a healthful indulgence. BELOW: Twisted, poached, baked, and packaged as gifts, fresh pretzels are irresistible.

soft pretzels

Homemade pretzels in a loaf pan make a welcome gift. Cut parchment as wide as the pan's length and long enough to wrap around pan and fold the ends over. Cut craft paper to that length, but half the width. Wrap papers around pan, and fold together. Punch holes, and tie with a ribbon.
MAKES 16

   1 tablespoon sugar
   1 tablespoon active dry yeast (one
      ¼-ounce envelope)
   5 to 6 cups all-purpose flour
   1 tablespoon salt
   2 teaspoons canola oil
   2 tablespoons baking soda
   1 large egg
   Coarse or pretzel salt
   Vegetable-oil cooking spray

1. Pour 2 cups warm water (about 110°) into the bowl of an electric mixer with dough hook. Add sugar, and stir to dissolve. Sprinkle with yeast; let sit 5 minutes; yeast should bubble.
2. Beat 1 cup flour into yeast on low until combined. Beat in salt and 4 cups flour until combined, about 30 seconds. Beat on medium-low until dough pulls away from sides of bowl, about 1½ minutes. Add ½ cup flour, and knead on low 1 minute more. If dough is still wet and sticky, add ½ cup more flour; knead until combined, about 30 seconds. Transfer to a lightly floured board, and knead about ten times until smooth.
3. Pour oil into a large bowl; swirl to coat sides. Transfer dough to bowl, turning to coat. Cover with a kitchen towel; leave in a warm spot for 1 hour, or until dough has doubled in size.
4. Heat oven to 450°. Lightly spray two baking sheets with cooking spray. Set aside. Punch down dough. Transfer to a lightly floured board. Knead once or twice, divide into sixteen pieces (about 2½ ounces each), and wrap in plastic.

5. Roll one piece of dough at a time into an 18-inch-long strip. Twist strip into pretzel shape; transfer dough to prepared baking sheet. Cover with a kitchen towel. Continue to form pretzels; eight will fit on each sheet. Let the dough rest until it rises slightly, about 15 minutes.
6. Meanwhile, fill large, shallow pot with 2 inches of water. Bring to a boil. Add baking soda. Reduce to simmer; transfer three to four pretzels to water. Poach one minute. Use slotted spoon to transfer pretzels to baking sheet. Continue until all pretzels are poached.
7. Beat egg with 1 tablespoon water. Brush pretzels with egg wash. Sprinkle with salt. Bake 12 to 15 minutes, until golden brown. Let cool on wire rack, or eat warm. Pretzels are best when eaten the same day, and will keep at room temperature, uncovered, for two days. Do not store in covered container.

hot chocolate

Why use a powder when perfect homemade hot chocolate is so simple? Omit the mint if you prefer plain hot chocolate.
SERVES 4

Mint Hot Chocolate
   4 cups milk
   6 sprigs fresh mint
   10 ounces semisweet or milk chocolate,
      cut into small pieces

1. Combine milk and mint sprigs in a saucepan, and scald the milk over medium-low heat. Remove from heat, and let stand covered for 5 to 10 minutes. Strain to remove mint leaves.
2. Return milk to saucepan; place over heat, add chocolate, and whisk until chocolate is completely melted and milk is frothy. Serve immediately.

Vanilla Hot Chocolate
   4 cups milk
   2 vanilla beans, split
   10 ounces semisweet or milk chocolate, cut
      into small pieces

1. Combine milk and split vanilla beans in a saucepan; scald the milk over medium-low heat. Remove from heat and take out the vanilla beans. Scrape the seeds from the beans into the milk, discarding the pods. Stir, then let stand covered for 5 to 10 minutes.
2. Return to medium-low heat, add chocolate, and whisk until chocolate is completely melted and milk is frothy. Serve immediately.

fruit butter

It's called fruit butter, but this thick spread doesn't contain an iota of fat—it's simply the essence of summer fruit.
MAKES ABOUT 2 CUPS

   3½ pounds fruit (such as peaches, plums, or
      apricots), pitted, peeled if desired, and
      cut into chunks
   1¼ cups sugar

1. Combine fruit, sugar, and 1 cup water in a saucepan over high heat. Bring to a boil, reduce heat, and cook for about 20 minutes, until fruit is very soft.
2. Purée the mixture, then return it to low heat. Cook, stirring frequently, until the mixture is thick and spreadable, 2 to 2½ hours.
3. Let cool, and transfer to airtight containers. Fruit butters will keep, refrigerated, for about one month, or frozen for up to three months.

balsamic strawberries

For a change from strawberry shortcake, try this classic Italian preparation. Balsamic vinegar *(aceto balsamico)*, the Italian vinegar from Modena, is aged in wood barrels for years, becoming sweet, tart, and deep, dark brown. Sprinkle it over sliced strawberries; its delicate acidity will bring out their flavor subtly. Spoon the strawberries over vanilla ice cream, or enjoy them on their own as a nonfat, low-calorie dessert. For the best results, use the oldest, best-quality balsamic vinegar you can find.

ice-cream sandwiches

These sweet little sandwiches let you re-create one of the joys of summer without chasing the ice-cream truck down the street. Let ice cream or sorbet soften at room temperature for fifteen minutes, then place a small scoop on one cookie, such as a Nilla wafer, French butter cookie, or Famous chocolate wafer. Top with another cookie; press together gently. If desired, roll sandwich through sprinkles to coat ice cream. Freeze on a baking sheet for an hour to harden, then wrap each sandwich in plastic wrap. Frozen, they keep for about a week—and are sure to be greeted with good humor.

summer slushes

The dog is under the porch, the kids are under the garden hose. Cold drinks are the first line of defense from the summer sun, and these frozen-fruit slushes come to the rescue with the perfect seasonal refreshment. Freeze peeled, seeded chunks of fruit or berries in sealed plastic bags. Zip the frozen fruit in a blender with a little water and sugar to taste.

melon margarita

This cool cocktail mixes the sweetness of watermelon with the tartness of a margarita. To make one, coat the rim of a glass with lime juice and dip it in salt. In a blender, combine the juice of 1½ limes, 3 tablespoons tequila, 1 tablespoon vodka, 1 teaspoon Triple Sec, 2 cups seeded watermelon flesh, ¼ cup sugar, and 3 cups crushed ice. Process until smooth; add another cup of ice, and blend until slushy. Pour into the glass, and serve.

rhubarb tea

As an alternative to summer's ubiquitous iced tea, try a pretty pink infusion of fresh rhubarb. Cut eight stalks of rhubarb into 3-inch lengths, add them to 8 cups of water, bring to a boil, and simmer for one hour. Strain the liquid, add sugar to taste (about a third of a cup), and let cool. Pour into glasses over ice, and garnish with a sprig of fresh mint.

coffee cubes

The first sip is just right, but it's not long before a glass of iced coffee is watery and weak. If the ice itself is made of coffee, it won't dilute your drink. Freeze freshly made coffee (or tea, for iced tea) in an ice-cube tray, then use the cubes to cool your brew.

cleaning clams

Sand is a pleasure on the beach, but it's quite another thing inside a bowl of freshly cooked shellfish. Before cooking, soak every twenty clams or mussels in 1½ gallons cold water with 1½ cups cornmeal for two hours. They will expel most of their ingested sand.

asparagus essentials

When you select them at the market, spears of asparagus should be crisp and green with tight, unopened tips—here's how to keep them that way. Asparagus is best eaten the day it's purchased, but it can be stored for up to three days. Wrap the bottom ends in damp paper towels, and seal in an airtight plastic bag *(top left)*; refrigerate in the crisper. Before cooking, snap the bottom off each spear; it breaks naturally just where it should. If the stalks are tough, peel the bottom third of each one. Here's one easy way to cook asparagus: Bind the spears into a bundle using kitchen string, and stand it on end in a few inches of boiling water in a small saucepan; invert another saucepan over the top for a lid. Cook until the stalks are just tender.

easy vinaigrette

A well-dressed salad rounds out almost any meal, so it's a good idea to keep an all-purpose vinaigrette on hand. Combine olive oil and balsamic or herb vinegar (three parts to one part) with salt, pepper, mustard, garlic, and herbs to taste. Transfer to a clean wine bottle and stop it with a new cork *(top center)*; the dressing will keep for weeks refrigerated. And this bottle is attractive enough to bring to the table.

cherries on ice

A bowl of cherries can languish in summer heat and sun. To keep cherries crisp and cool, mix them with ice cubes or crushed ice *(middle left)*; replenish the supply as it melts.

tearless onions

At last, no more tears—or stinging, burning eyes—while chopping onions. Cut them near a flame *(middle center)*, and the gaseous sulfur compounds released from onions will burn off before they irritate your eyes. Don't forget to turn off the stove when you're finished. Or try lighting a votive candle near the cutting board instead.

pastry bites

Scraps of dough that usually get left by the wayside can be turned into delectable little treats *(middle right)*. Be imaginative: Braid, twist, or tie the dough in knots, and sprinkle them with sugar and cinnamon. Or pinch the sides of a circle into a cup, and drop a dollop of jam into it, making a tiny tart. Since they only take ten minutes to bake (remove them from the oven as soon as they turn golden), you can be nibbling on them while the pie's still in the oven.

kitchen tips

serving lobster

They may come from the water, but lobsters shouldn't be filled with it, too. After boiling or steaming a lobster, cut the tip off each claw with kitchen shears, and hold the lobster up by the tail *(top right)*, allowing the liquid to drain out before you crack the shell.

herb rack

A nest of herbs can serve as an impromptu roasting rack and infuse the meat with flavor at the same time. Arrange sage, thyme, or other stalks in a roasting pan, and place meat on top *(bottom center and right)*. Large, woodier stalks, such as the ones in the garden at the end of the summer, work best.

cutting julienne

Vegetables for salads, stir-fries, and garnishes are often julienned, or sliced into matchsticks. Start by cutting a vegetable into very thin slices. Stack several slices, and slice again *(top left)*. Cut the matchsticks into the length you need.

dicing

It's essential that diced vegetables be uniform in size so they cook evenly—and look good, too. Slice the vegetable very thin; stack several flat slices, and slice again very thin, into julienne. Gather several matchsticks *(top center)* and chop into equal-size cubes.

chopping an onion

Here is the easiest, most efficient way to chop an onion. Cut it in half from top to bottom; slice off stem ends. Remove skin. Make vertical cuts lengthwise, along the veins of the onion, without cutting through the root end—it holds the onion together as you work. Make a few horizontal cuts from cut edge toward root end, then chop across onion, resulting in dice *(top right)*. This technique can also be used on garlic cloves and shallots.

preserving herbs

With this technique, suggested by chef and author Giuliano Bugialli, you can store your summer crop of fresh aromatic herbs like basil, rosemary, and sage. In a glass container, alternate half-inch layers of kosher salt with single layers of herbs *(middle center)*, beginning and ending with salt. The salt absorbs mold-breeding moisture and inhibits enzymes that turn fresh herbs brown. Use the herbs within six months—and it won't be long before they're growing in the garden again.

keeping berries fresh

Ripe berries are so tender they burst in your mouth—if they don't get squashed in the carton first. To keep them undamaged, lay them in a single layer on a baking sheet lined with paper towels *(middle right)*. Cover loosely with plastic wrap; refrigerate until you're ready to wash and eat them—which should be as soon as possible. Rinse the berries very lightly; a strong dousing washes away their flavor and perfume.

kitchen tips

chiffonades

Thin strips of herbs or leafy vegetables are called chiffonade, which means "made of rags" in French. The strips make a pretty garnish, and sliced this way, the leaves don't get crushed or bruised. Stack several leaves, like basil *(middle left)*, with the largest on the bottom, and roll them up from one side to the other. Slice into ribbons.

a clean slice

In the kitchen, dental floss can do the job of a sharp knife—and with better results. Stretched taut between your hands, a length of floss or fishing line splits a cake *(bottom center)* into layers with ease. It will also slice a log of soft, fresh cheese *(bottom right)* into rounds that stay intact instead of crumbling.

celebrating

[confections, cookies, decorations]

Each holiday has its distinct, special history, but whether it's Easter or Thanksgiving, Christmas or Hanukkah, the focus remains on celebrating with family and friends. The baking and decorating ideas in this chapter can help you do just that, and you may find that you'll want to add many of them to your own favorite traditions.

You can expand holidays well beyond the days themselves by making your preparations part of the celebration. Turn the kitchen into a workshop for an afternoon, drape the house in decorations with family, and invite friends to join you. It's like starting the party early. Or on the day itself, surprise someone with a handwritten valentine, a single Easter egg, or homemade Halloween treats.

But you don't have to wait for a special occasion. Many ideas here are adaptable to birthdays, other holidays, or any day in between. When you take the time to appreciate small accomplishments and great pleasures, any day can be a celebration.

Opposite: So what if they don't say "Be Mine"? These heart-shaped lollipops certainly get their message across. Flavored with lemon, vanilla, or coffee, they are more subtle and sophisticated than the pops you remember from childhood; a bit of citrus peel, a slice of dried fig, or a coffee bean is suspended in each one.

lollipop hearts

The molds for these pops can be mail-ordered (see the Guide), or you can create them yourself. To do so, snip through the bottoms of inexpensive metal cookie cutters and bend them into hearts. Or make molds from 20-gauge aluminum sheeting (available at hardware stores). With heavy shears, cut metal into ¾-inch-wide strips, 6 inches to 10 inches long; use blade edge to bend corners and shape into hearts. With masking tape, secure a lollipop stick in the opening of each heart. Brush corn oil onto molds and onto a piece of waxed paper set on a baking sheet. Place molds on the paper. To make 12 to 15 pops: In a saucepan, combine 1 cup sugar, ½ cup honey, and 6 tablespoons water. Cook until mixture reaches 300° on a candy thermometer, then set pan in a bowl of cool water. Mix in 1 teaspoon lemon, vanilla, or coffee extract. Place a piece of candied lemon peel, a coffee bean, or a slice of dried fig or pear in each mold and fill to ¼ inch with the caramelized sugar. Cool pops for 30 minutes. If desired, wrap each pop loosely in cellophane and bind it around with a piece of seam binding or ribbon.

valentine fortunes

Take romantic destiny into your own hands with these oversize fortune cookies, made from a classic French butter-cookie recipe.
MAKES 15

Nonstick cooking spray
5 tablespoons unsalted butter
4 large egg whites
1 cup superfine sugar
1 cup all-purpose flour, sifted
Pinch of salt
3 tablespoons heavy cream
1 teaspoon almond extract

1. Heat oven to 400°. Coat a baking sheet well with cooking spray. Melt butter in a small saucepan over low heat.

2. In bowl of an electric mixer, combine egg whites and sugar; beat on medium speed for about 30 seconds. Add flour and salt; beat to combine. Add butter, heavy cream, and almond extract; beat to combine, 30 seconds.

3. Pour 1 tablespoon batter onto half the baking sheet; spread with a spoon into a thin 5-inch circle *(above left)*; repeat on other half of sheet. Bake until edges turn golden, about 8 minutes.

4. Place baking sheet on a heat-resistant surface. Working quickly, slide a spatula (an offset spatula works best) under one cookie. Lift, and place on a dish towel. Fold cookie in half, pinching at top to form loose semicircle *(above center)*. Insert index fingers into ends; press indentation into center of cookie while bending ends together to form shape of a fortune cookie *(above right)*. This process should take about 10 seconds; once the cookie hardens you cannot fold it. Repeat with other cookie. Continue until all batter is used up. To avoid wasting batter, try shaping a circle of paper first.

5. Using a white wax pencil, write your Valentine messages on long strips of sturdy art paper, such as the Japanese moriki shown here. Thread fortunes through the cooled cookies.

ABOVE: With various decorating techniques, heart cookies can be iced and sugared with dots, plaids, letters, and lacy designs. RIGHT: Chocolate, gingerbread, and sugar cookies edged with tinted sugar. BELOW, FROM LEFT: Tinted sugar crystals adhere to the cookies where egg white has been applied with a paintbrush.

gingerbread cookies

This recipe is for large cookies, like the fluted hearts on the opposite page, which are almost eight inches tall. When making oversize cookies, use two spatulas to transfer the dough to the baking pan. Bake and cool the cookies before decorating them. Hearts are perfect for Valentine's Day, but the versatile decorating techniques that follow can be used on cookies for any occasion.
MAKES ABOUT 16 LARGE COOKIES

    6 cups sifted all-purpose flour
    1 teaspoon baking soda
    ½ teaspoon baking powder
    ½ pound (2 sticks) unsalted butter
    1 cup dark-brown sugar, packed
    4 teaspoons ground ginger
    4 teaspoons ground cinnamon
    1½ teaspoons ground cloves
    ¼ teaspoon finely ground black pepper
    1½ teaspoons salt
    2 large eggs
    1 cup unsulfered molasses

1. In a large bowl, sift together flour, baking soda, and baking powder.
2. In an electric mixer, cream butter and sugar until fluffy. Mix in spices and salt, then eggs and molasses. Add flour mixture; combine on low speed. Divide dough in thirds; wrap in plastic. Chill for at least 1 hour.
3. Heat oven to 350°. On a floured work surface, roll dough ⅛ inch thick. Cut into desired shapes. Transfer to ungreased baking sheets; refrigerate until firm, 15 minutes. Bake cookies 8 to 10 minutes, or until crisp but not darkened. Let cookies cool on wire racks, then decorate as desired.

sugar cookies

These cookies can also be cut into any shape and decorated for any occasion. For chocolate cookies, see page 63.
MAKES ABOUT 16 LARGE COOKIES

    4 cups sifted all-purpose flour
    ½ teaspoon salt
    1 teaspoon baking powder
    ½ pound (2 sticks) unsalted butter
    2 cups sugar
    2 large eggs
    2 teaspoons pure vanilla extract *or* fresh
       lemon juice and zest of lemons

1. In a large bowl, sift together flour, salt, and baking powder.
2. Use an electric mixer to cream butter and sugar until fluffy. Beat in eggs.
3. Add flour mixture; mix on low speed until thoroughly combined. Stir in vanilla or lemon juice and zest. Wrap dough in plastic; chill for 30 minutes.
4. Heat oven to 325°. On a floured surface, roll dough to ⅛ inch thick. Cut into desired shapes. Transfer to ungreased baking sheets; refrigerate until firm, 15 minutes. Bake 8 to 10 minutes, or until edges just start to brown. Cool on wire racks; decorate as desired.

royal icing

For an especially glossy icing, mix in a few drops of glycerin (available at drugstores).
MAKES ABOUT 2½ CUPS

    2 large egg whites, or more to thin icing
    4 cups sifted confectioners' sugar, or more
       to thicken icing
       Juice of 1 lemon
    3 drops glycerin (optional)

Beat the egg whites until stiff but not dry. Add sugar, lemon juice, and glycerin (if using); beat for 1 minute more. If icing is too thick, add more egg whites; if it is too thin, add more sugar.

Note: Raw eggs should not be used in food for pregnant women, babies, young children, or anyone whose health is compromised. Meringue powder, prepared according to package instructions, can be used instead of egg whites.

decorating techniques

Icing
Use liquid or paste food colors to tint the icing, or leave it plain white. Pipe the icing using a pastry bag fitted with a small round tip (#1, 1.5, or 2) onto the cookies freehand, or outline an area and fill it in. Don't apply icing too close to the edge of the cookies; it may spread. Let the cookies dry overnight.

Sugaring
This simple technique can create plaids, stripes, borders, or other designs.
1. Sugar crystals come in a variety of sizes. To tint crystals, use a toothpick to dab powdered food coloring into sugar. Start with a little; add more as needed. Blend colors for the shade you want.
2. Whisk together two egg whites, or use meringue powder if you're concerned about consuming raw eggs. Dip a new, good-quality paintbrush or a pastry brush into egg white and paint it onto a cookie in the design you want.
3. Sprinkle sugar generously over egg white; let stand for 30 minutes to dry. Shake or gently brush off any stray sugar. For plaids, complete all the stripes in one direction first, let dry, then make stripes in the opposite direction, painting egg white directly over first stripes.

Flocking
This technique uses sugar and royal icing; tint them as described above. Pipe icing onto cookies, and spoon sugar over wet icing. Let dry for 30 minutes, shake off extra sugar, and let dry overnight.

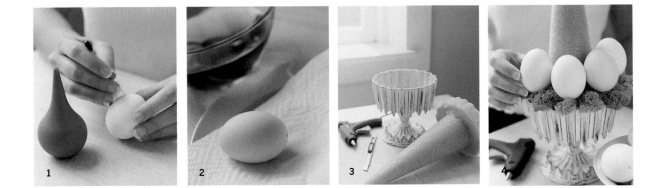

egg topiary

An Easter bunny trained in English gardening might have invented these trim topiaries *(opposite)*. To make the yellow topiary, you'll need 7 extra-large, 7 large, and 8 small eggs.

1. Poke a hole into the bottom and side of each; blow out the insides with an egg-blowing tool or a rubber ear syringe, available at pharmacies. Rinse shells and let dry completely.

2. Bring 3 cups water to a boil and remove from heat; add 2 tablespoons white vinegar and 2 or 3 drops of food coloring, or more for a deeper color. Dye the eggs until they reach the desired shade. Let dry completely.

3. Cut a sheet of floral foam, available from florists, to fit an urn or other container. Using a hot-glue gun, attach a 6-inch cone of floral foam to the foam base (trim the cone, if necessary).

4. Hot-glue dried reindeer moss, available from florists, to the base. Hot-glue the 7 extra-large eggs to the cone so that the holes are facing inward and the eggs tilt outward slightly. Tuck moss between the eggs. Hot-glue a layer of 6 large eggs above the first row. Still angling the eggs outward and adding moss after each row, hot-glue a row of 5 and a row of 3 small eggs, reserving 1 large egg for the top.

To make the blue topiary, follow the above steps, using eggs dyed blue, Spanish moss, and an 8-inch cone. Keep the eggs upright as you glue them.

egg ornaments

In Europe, Easter eggs are often hung on tree branches and bushes. Bring this custom into your home with these eggs, embellished with ribbon and trimmings. Begin by blowing out, rinsing, and dying eggs as described for the egg topiary. Attach a band of ribbon or rickrack around the shell with clear-drying craft glue. Cover the hole in one end of the egg with a silk flower or a small bow; glue in place. Put a pearl-tipped pin through a ribbon loop, insert into other end, and glue pin in place. Hang the eggs from an arrangement of flowering branches.

egg stenciling

Tired of the same old solid-color eggs? Try these punctuation marks, letters, plaids, and polka dots *(opposite)*.

1. To make a plaid egg, begin with a white hard-boiled egg or dye one a solid, pale color, as for the egg topiary. Band the egg lengthwise with ¼-inch-wide masking tape, repositioning as necessary to get a tight fit. Firmly rub the tape with your fingernail or a burnishing tool from an art-supply store so that dye can't seep underneath.
2. Dip egg into your chosen dye, raising and dipping until the color deepens as desired. Blot egg with a paper towel. Let dry ten minutes. Remove tape.
3. Band the egg's width with tape at its widest point; repeat to make smaller circles around each end. Burnish, dye, and dry as before.
4. Remove tape.
5. You can also follow this dyeing method with stick-on dots and press-on vinyl type, both available at art-supply or office-supply stores. The waterproof vinyl type works especially well; periods make great little polka dots, too.

flowered basket

The Easter basket is forever being shown up by the eggs it holds. To make a basket as special as its contents, try dressing it up with silk flowers and leaves, available in most craft shops. A hot-glue gun is indispensable for this project. Begin by lining an inexpensive basket with a circle of satin or silk three times its diameter, tucking and hot-gluing it into place. Next, hot-glue the end of a length of seam binding at one handle end; wrap the handle with the seam binding and hot-glue at the other end. Remove the stems from artificial flowers (you'll need about sixty for a medium-size basket, five or six inches in diameter) and hot-glue the buds onto the basket, covering its entire surface. With leaves, work from the top down. If you are using multilayered flowers like the pink ranunculuses *(below right)*, you can pare down some buds to make a variety of sizes.

paper baskets

These pastel paper bags decorated with construction paper are a whimsical alternative to traditional woven baskets that usually hold all of your Easter treasures. Fold down the top of each bag four times to make a 1½-inch-wide band. Trace flowers and leaves onto paper (see templates on page 139); cut them out with a utility knife.

1. Using an ⅛-inch hole punch, pierce the center of each flower, the base of each leaf, and the front or the band of the bag. Arrange flowers and leaves on bag so that all the holes line up. Push a metal eyelet, available in kits from sewing stores, through the holes from the outside of the bag in.

2. Insert the small post included in the kit into the back of the eyelet; hammer until eyelet flattens. Punch holes in the band at each end and fit them with eyelets. Lace a 2-foot length of 2-inch-wide wired ribbon through holes; knot to secure, and trim ends.

crystallized flowers

Icing can masquerade as flowers, but when the garden's blooming, why not use the real thing? Edible flowers can be crystallized, then scattered across cakes or cupcakes. Try pansies, Johnny-jump-ups, violets, roses, for-get-me-nots, cornflowers, and scented-geranium leaves. The technique—sealing the flowers in a thin coating of egg white and sugar—isn't difficult, but it does take patience and practice. Assemble the supplies before you pick the blossoms, and make sure to choose an edible variety. Pick extras, since they won't all be perfect. Cut the stem close to the base of the flower. Dilute an egg white or powdered egg whites with water. Hold a blossom with surgical tweezers and brush the egg-white mixture on all surfaces of the flower with a watercolor paint-brush. Then sprinkle superfine sugar over the entire flower. Handling it carefully, place the flower on a tray covered with waxed paper and set in a warm, dry place for two to four days, until crisp. Larger flowers, like pansies and roses, need to be turned regularly so moisture doesn't collect beneath them and all surfaces dry evenly. It's a good idea to make more crystallized flowers than you need—they will keep for months in a dry place.

openwork pumpkins

Pierced creamware dishes, a staple of the English table in the eighteenth century, were the inspiration for these carved gourds *(opposite)*. With careful carving, you can mimic the pottery's lacy designs.

1. Select a pumpkin or squash such as *(from left)* Lumina, spaghetti squash, and Blue Hubbard. Assemble your tools. Hardware and art-supply stores sell reasonably priced sets of wood-carving tools. Other items, such as small pieces of pipe, can also be used to make cuts. When choosing tools, imagine the design you'll carve. Bear in mind the shape of the perforation the tool will make, and choose tools that will produce unusual punctures. For example, top and bottom incisions made with a V-shaped gouge leave a diamond form.

2. Cut an opening in the bottom of your gourd. Scrape out the seeds and most of the flesh. Place a length of masking tape around the circumference of the gourd for a carving guideline. Start cutting.

3. The going gets easier once you've circled the gourd with a pattern—just keep following it, adding more bands of cuts. If you carve a small, simple design, make an air hole on one side to help the candle burn.

apple votives

A flotilla of apples bobbing in a steel tub evokes memories of headlong dunks into icy water. Carved into holiday candleholders, they are a prize for the eyes alone. Every apple will float differently, so see how they balance in water before marking their tops with a dot. Place a tea light over the dot, and trace around its circumference with a utility knife, inserting the knife vertically as deep as the tea light is tall. Set aside the light, cut the circle into sections, and scoop them out with a spoon. Squeeze lemon juice onto the cut surface to keep the apple from turning brown. Insert a tea light. Just before guests or trick-or-treaters arrive, float the little lanterns in a basin of water, and set their wicks aglow.

RIGHT: These dark-chocolate peanut-butter cups are delicious homemade versions of a classic Halloween treat. BELOW RIGHT: Decorated using a technique called webbing, gingerbread cookies look like spiders in their webs, and the chocolate cookie takes the guise of a spooky bat. BELOW, TOP TO BOTTOM: Webbing a sugar cookie with white and brown royal icing.

chocolate cookies

To form cookies into bats and cobwebs, use a cookie cutter or cut out a cardboard template in the desired shape; place the template on the dough and cut around it with the point of a sharp knife. Bake and cool. Additional cookie recipes are on page 53.

MAKES ABOUT 16 LARGE OR 2½ DOZEN SMALLER COOKIES

3 cups sifted all-purpose flour
1¼ cups unsweetened cocoa
¼ teaspoon salt
½ teaspoon ground cinnamon
¾ pound (3 sticks) unsalted butter
2½ cups sifted confectioners' sugar
2 large eggs, lightly beaten
1 teaspoon pure vanilla extract

1. In a large bowl, sift together flour, cocoa, salt, and cinnamon. Set aside.
2. Use an electric mixer to cream butter and sugar until fluffy. Beat in eggs and vanilla.
3. Add flour mixture; mix on low speed until thoroughly combined. Divide dough in half; wrap in plastic. Chill at least 1 hour.
4. Heat oven to 350°. On a floured surface, roll dough to ⅛ inch thick. Cut into desired shapes. Transfer to ungreased baking sheets; refrigerate until firm, 15 minutes. Bake 8 to 10 minutes, until crisp but not darkened. Cool on wire racks; decorate as desired.

decorating technique

Webbing

Decorate the cookies with royal icing (white and black or dark brown; use liquid food coloring to tint it, see page 53 for recipe) and a technique known as webbing. To make the cobweb: Spoon white icing onto the center of the cookie and smooth with a small spatula. While the icing is still wet, pipe a spiral of black icing from the center to the outer edge of the cookie. Drag a knife point from the center of the spiral to the points on the edge of the cookie. Clean the knife, then drag it in the opposite direction from the middle of each curve at the edge of the cookie toward the center. Finish off the cobweb by placing dots of black icing on the points of the web. To add a spider, draw a center blob in icing, with legs radiating out of it.

The webbing technique can be adapted to create the bat as well. Draw four icing lines in an arc on each wing, then drag the knife point across the width in alternating directions.

peanut-butter cups

For the most delicious results, make these using good-quality chocolate and natural peanut butter.

MAKES 36

2 cups sifted confectioners' sugar
1½ cups smooth peanut butter, preferably all-natural
3 tablespoons unsalted butter
1 pound bittersweet or semisweet chocolate
36 1⅜-inch paper candy cups

1. Combine sugar, peanut butter, and butter in an electric mixer fitted with a paddle attachment. Beat on medium-low speed until combined. Transfer mixture to a pastry bag fitted with a ½-inch plain tip, and set aside.
2. Melt the chocolate in a double boiler over simmering water. Keep melted chocolate over hot water near work area. Use a small spoon or paintbrush to coat insides of the paper candy cups with the melted chocolate, making sure to cover bottom and sides well. Transfer cups to a rimmed baking sheet or muffin tins (which will keep the cups from sliding around). Transfer to freezer until set, about 10 minutes.
3. Remove cold chocolate cups from freezer. Pipe peanut-butter filling into each cup until three-quarters full. Spoon melted chocolate into each cup to cover. Return to freezer until set, 15 to 25 minutes. Serve right away, or keep tightly sealed in the freezer for 2 to 3 days. To serve, remove from freezer, peel off paper, and eat cold.

ABOVE: Individual Bundt spice cakes covered in marzipan are a sweet way to celebrate autumn. RIGHT: Making the pumpkins' marzipan shells, and cutting and shaping their leaves and stems.

pumpkin cakes

Miniature Bundt pans produce these pumpkin-shaped cakes; cover them in orange marzipan and top with marzipan stems to celebrate Halloween or Thanksgiving.
MAKES 6 CAKES

    4 tablespoons unsalted butter, softened,
        plus 1 tablespoon for the pan
    2 ounces fresh ginger, peeled and sliced
        into ½-inch pieces
    ½ cup dark molasses
    ½ teaspoon baking soda
    1¼ cups all-purpose flour
    1¼ teaspoon salt
    1 teaspoon ground ginger
    ¾ teaspoon ground cinnamon
        Pinch ground cloves
    1½ teaspoons baking powder
    ½ cup packed light brown sugar
    1 large egg
    ¾ cup canned pumpkin purée
    2 pounds 3 ounces Marzipan (recipe follows)
        Nonstick vegetable oil spray

1. Heat oven to 350°. Using a pastry brush, coat interiors of 6 mini Bundt pans and a 12-by-18-inch piece of aluminum foil with 1 tablespoon softened butter. Set aside.

2. Place fresh ginger and ¾ cup hot tap water in small saucepan; bring to a boil. Reduce heat to low; simmer until reduced to ½ cup, 10 to 15 minutes. Remove from heat; strain into a bowl, discarding ginger. Add molasses and baking soda to liquid. Set aside.

3. Sift together flour, salt, ground ginger, cinnamon, ground cloves, and baking powder. Set aside.

4. With electric mixer on medium-high speed, whip remaining 4 tablespoons butter and brown sugar together until light and creamy, about 5 minutes. Add egg and beat until fluffy, about 5 minutes. Reduce to low speed and add pumpkin purée until just incorporated. Alternately add one quarter of dry ingredients and one-third of molasses mixture, ending with dry ingredients. Mix on low speed, scraping bowl after each addition, until incorporated. Fill Bundt pans halfway with mixture.

5. Place Bundt pans in oven and bake for 20 minutes. Remove from oven and place on a cooling rack for ½ hour.

6. Invert Bundt pans onto a sheet pan; tap firmly several times on hard surface to release cakes.

7. To form marzipan coatings, spray the interiors of clean Bundt pans with nonstick vegetable oil spray. Divide the orange-colored marzipan into 6 equal pieces; roll out each to a 5-inch-diameter circle, ¼-inch thick. Place marzipan circles into each pan, covering insides. Press gently over core and down along the core's sides, covering each form completely. Press into indentations, being careful not to thin the marzipan by pressing too hard.

8. Transfer Bundt pans to freezer for 30 minutes. Remove pans from freezer and lift out marzipan and place on cake, matching indentations for a secure fit. With cake in one hand, gently tuck bottom edge of marzipan under cake, to form a smooth edge. Repeat with remaining cakes.

9. Take prepared stems and place into center hole of each cake. Serve on top of marzipan leaves within 6 hours.

marzipan

This soft confection is like artist's clay, capable of assuming many shapes and colors found in nature.
MAKES 2 POUNDS 3 OUNCES

    1 pound almond paste
    1 pound confectioners' sugar
    ⅓ cup Karo light corn syrup or 3 egg whites
        Paste food colorings: sunset orange, red,
        egg shade, juniper or moss green, and
        brown
    ½ teaspoon cinnamon
        Confectioners' sugar for dusting board, if
        necessary

1. Combine confectioners' sugar and almond paste in food processor; process until smooth, about 3 minutes.

2. Add corn syrup or egg whites; process about 1 minute until well-combined. Remove from processor, cover with plastic wrap, and set aside for an hour at room temperature.

3. Divide marzipan equally—half to cover pumpkins, half for stems and leaves. To color covers, dip a clean toothpick in sunset orange and egg shade, then dab marzipan. Add cinnamon; knead on a cutting board, adding small amounts of coloring, if necessary, to achieve desired color. Wrap well with plastic wrap, and set aside.

4. Divide remaining marzipan equally—half for stems, half for leaves. For stems, divide marzipan in half again. Using a toothpick for each color, dab half with juniper or moss-green coloring. Knead, adding more color if necessary to achieve desired shade. Mix uncolored marzipan with juniper marzipan for marbled effect; divide into 6 equal parts. Roll with fingertips to create 6 stems. If marzipan gets sticky, dust with sugar. Score stems with a knife 6 or 7 times, then curl ends. Let sit for 1 hour to firm up before placing on cakes.

5. For leaves, divide remaining marzipan into 3 equal pieces. Color one piece with egg shade; one red and brown; one juniper or moss green. Blend 3 marzipan pieces into a ball; flatten with a rolling pin until it has a marbled effect, about ⅛-inch thick. Use cookie or gum-paste cutters to cut out leaves. Press "veiner" mold (see the Guide) onto leaf shapes. For a natural, rounded form, dry leaves along inside curve of a glass bowl or rest on edge of a sheet pan.

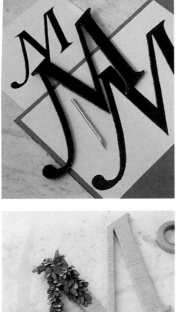

monogram wreath

Nearly two thousand years ago, the Romans created lush topiaries to spell out the names of their leaders. This monogram wreath *(opposite)*, fashioned from evergreen branch tips, revisits that tradition. It has all the charm of a topiary but without the usual clipping and trimming. And it also proves that wreaths don't have to be shaped like the letter O.

To make it, start by choosing a letter style you like from a book of typography, or design a letter yourself. On a photocopier, enlarge the letter to the wreath size you want; this one is about 12 inches tall. Use spray adhesive to join two pieces of corrugated cardboard, then glue the letter to the cardboard. With a utility knife, cut out the letter; this will be the form for the wreath. Wrap the form in green floral tape to mask any gaps in the greenery. We used boxwood, which is sturdy and relatively long lasting, but other evergreens can be used. Take a small bundle of 2-to-3-inch branch tips, and place them on the form at a good starting point. Wrap floral wire around bottom of the stems and secure to the form; do not cut wire. Add another bundle of tips, overlapping first by about half, and wire it. Continue overlapping bundles until front of form is covered, then cut wire and twist to secure. Hang finished wreath with ribbon or fishing line, or on a hook.

evergreen bobeches

Here's a much less formal, much more festive version of bobeches, those little collars meant to catch dripping candle wax. To make them, form a circle of 18-gauge wire just larger than the candle you intend to use. Choose evergreen leaves, bay-laurel leaves, or boxwood or juniper branch tips of relatively even scale and size. To attach the branch tips to wire circles, you'll need 12 to 18 inches of 22-gauge floral wire per bobeche. Begin by attaching one leaf or tip to the wire circle by wrapping together with floral wire. Without cutting the floral wire, add another evergreen piece, overlapping the first, and wrap with wire to secure. Repeat, completely covering the circle. Cut the floral wire, and twist it to secure.

gift bags

A few artful techniques can be used to transform plain paper bags into custom-made gift wrap, especially convenient for odd-shaped, hard-to-wrap gifts.
1. Use a hole punch to make two small holes in the bag's flap. Poke a sprig of juniper or other greens through the holes to secure the flap, and tie a ribbon around it.
2. Seal the bag with vintage holiday stamps, and tie with string.
3. Make lengthwise slits along the flap of the bag and lace ribbon through. Knot each ribbon end.

4. Stitch two pretty buttons to a bag, and wind a length of colorful twine between them.
5. Make two buttonholes in ribbon so that when it's draped over a folded bag, the buttonholes line up on the front and back; cut a small hole in the bag where the buttonholes fall, and secure with a cuff link. Glue the ends of the ribbon to bottom of bag.
6. Make two holes in the flap of a bag, and lace ribbon through from the back. Tie a millinery fruit or other small, decorative object into the knot.

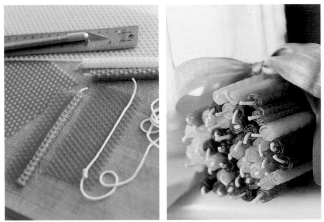

rolled hanukkah candles

Many Hanukkah candles are colored like crayons; these subtle alternatives are made of beeswax sheets, which come in the loveliest of colors. Look for the wax at candle-making-supply houses and craft stores. Slice wax sheets into 2-by-4½-inch rectangles. Cut wicking to 5½-inch lengths; knot one end. Warm a piece of wax with a blow dryer until just pliable, 10 to 15 seconds. Lay wicking along edge so it overhangs one end. Roll wax tightly around wicking; press seam with your finger to smooth. Make a set for yourself, and more as gifts. Over the eight days of the holiday, forty-four candles are lit.

silver-cup menorah

As the focal point in the observation of Hanukkah, the Festival of Lights, the menorah deserves special attention. Instead of the traditional candelabrum, try a row of eight silver cups to hold the candles that are lit each evening of the holiday, along with a ninth for the shamas, the candle that kindles the others. Look for the cups at antique shops and flea markets. Fill them with enough sand to keep candles upright.

snow lanterns

These fire-and-ice decorations will actually make you long for snow. Placed on the front porch, they provide a warm welcome for your guests on chilly winter evenings.

1. To make the dramatic snowball sculptures, start by propping a 40-watt outdoor light fixture in a jelly jar or glass tumbler. Place it in a wide-mouthed bucket or other container; we used cast-iron urns.

2. Make equal-size, tightly packed snowballs. Use them to build a pyramid around the bulb, with the container as a base.

3. To make the smaller snow lanterns, fill a bucket with snow, then hollow it out, leaving a shell. Pack the snow shell thoroughly, then carefully unmold it from the bucket. Spray the shell with water to solidify, and place jelly jar or glass tumbler inside to hold a candle.

paper decorations

Christmas is about tradition, but there's always room for a few new decorating and wrapping ideas. And with these techniques using paper, you might just start some new traditions.

1. For paper bows, cut medium-weight paper into strips, or use quilling paper, which comes in strips. For the pink and red bows, fold strips of paper into loops; add dabs of glue where the paper meets. For the green bow, curl ends of paper strips by winding them around a smooth-sided pen; glue strips together at their centers.

2. Christmas crackers are an old European tradition. Two people grasp the ends and tug until the package opens and a prize comes tumbling out. You can make your own crackers to use as placecards for your holiday table. Roll a piece of cardboard into a tube and secure with tape; put a gift, such as a refrigerator magnet, candy, or a tiny toy, inside. Wrap the tube in tissue paper and tie the ends with ribbon. Add a label if you wish.

3. and **4.** Plain self-adhesive dots, a stationery-store staple, can become cheerful garlands for the tree or mantle. Working in a well-ventilated area, color dots with wide felt-tip markers. Stick them, back to back, onto button thread. Make a few extra dots and stick them to tissue-paper-wrapped gifts.

5. As the countdown to Christmas begins, add to the excitement with a takeoff on the advent calendar: advent gifts. Wrap up twenty-five small gifts and give each one a number instead of a name tag. Tuck them into a stair railing, or scatter them throughout the house and let family members take turns finding them.

giving

[ribbons, wraps, handmade presents]

Think of the best presents you've ever received. Chances are they weren't the most expensive ones. Gifts that are thoughtful and inventive are always more appreciated than those that are extravagant and exorbitant.

There is an art to giving, which only begins with choosing the gift itself. Instead of scouring stores, search your imagination. If you've never thought of making a gift before, here is a whole range of projects for any level of skill. You can tailor each idea to the recipient's tastes and interests. Or consider having a simple present engraved or embroidered with a monogram or message; it will instantly become a special keepsake.

Remember, too, that holidays and birthdays aren't the only times for giving. Use small, handmade presents to say thank you, celebrate a change of season, or welcome dinner guests, houseguests, or new neighbors.

Once you've selected a gift, turn your attention to packing and wrapping it. Splurge on an opulent box or indulge in a length of lovely silk ribbon. Beautiful adornments immeasurably enhance a well-chosen present, and they also become part of the present itself, to be used again and again.

Opposite: These small pillows have a surprisingly regal provenance. Filled with lavender, they are similiar to those made for European aristocracy in the Middle Ages, when the fragrant herb was a rare luxury. Silk taffeta hits the right note of indulgence for a special gift—and you won't need much more than a swatch of fabric.

lavender pillows

The first step in making the lavender pillows on page 72 is choosing the size; the smallest pillow shown is 4 inches square; the largest is 7 by 15 inches. Cut two pieces of fabric to the same size. With right sides facing, sew the pieces together, leaving a 2-to-3-inch opening on one side. Clip the corners, and turn the fabric right side out. Fill the pillow with lavender or a mix of lavender and flax seeds, in any ratio. Flax seeds, which have the texture of small, soft pebbles, are available at health-food stores. Stitch up the opening. These pretty cushions are charming as throw pillows or sachets; their gravelly texture and refreshing scent makes them appealing as neck rolls and eye pillows as well.

paperwhite bundle

In the winter, give a gift that grows. Paperwhites, indoor bulbs that produce fragrant flowers, can be planted in the months of November, December, and January. Bundle together bulbs, pebbles, and a decorative container; wrap them in a square of fabric and bind with a ribbon. A narrow glass vase shows off one blossom; more bulbs can be planted in a wider container. Don't forget to include these instructions: Place bulbs an inch apart in pebbles, leaving top third of bulb exposed; add water to cover bottoms of bulbs. Place in a cool, well-lit spot until shoots are 4 inches high. Move to a sunny windowsill; water regularly. In 4 to 6 weeks, flowers will appear.

ribbon boxes

Covered completely in ribbons and trimmings, these gift boxes are worthy of being presents themselves. To make the flower-topped box, glue grosgrain ribbon around the sides of a box and lid; glue fabric millinery flowers to top.

The basket-weave box begins with a square white box and white grosgrain ribbon in a width that divides evenly into one of the box's sides. Cut pieces of ribbon long enough to extend from inside the rim of the box, down one side, across the bottom, and up the opposite side. Glue ribbons side by side inside the rim of one side of the box. Wrap them smoothly down the side, across the bottom, and up the other side, gluing the loose ends inside the opposite rim. Using a second set of ribbons, weave the bottom of the box first, one ribbon at a time, under and over attached ribbons, pulling the ends up the two remaining bare sides and gluing them inside the box. Now cut lengths of ribbon equal to perimeter of the box plus 1 inch, and weave horizontally around the box, gluing the ends beneath a vertical ribbon. Weave the lid in the same fashion.

The round box is bound in a single piece of satin ribbon, which is attached with tape to the center of the lid, then wrapped in overlapping circles around the box. The end is looped into four gentle folds and secured on top with a pearl-tipped hat pin.

blooming bow

Bound into a bow, a flower in bloom enlivens any wrapped gift. This peony's stem is tucked into a plastic vial with a rubber top. Wrap the vial in ribbon, then tie it to the ribbon that binds the package. A little vial holds enough water to keep a flower looking fresh for several hours, so attach the bloom to the gift shortly before presenting it.

button-topped box

Making a button-covered box is a good way to put a supply of these decorative orphans to use. Begin with a small white cardboard box with a detachable lid. Starting at the center of the lid and working out to the edges, glue buttons side by side to completely cover the top of the lid; use clear-drying, all-purpose glue. On the sides of the lid, finish with a few rows of buttons that overlap the edges. For the bottom part of the box, use ribbon that is the same width as the box. Cut two lengths of ribbon long enough to extend from inside the rim of the box, down one side, across the bottom, up the opposite side, and inside the opposite rim. Glue one ribbon inside the rim of one side of the box. Wrap it smoothly down the side, across the bottom, and up the other side, gluing the loose end inside the opposite rim. To finish, repeat with other piece of ribbon on remaining sides.

finishing a ribbon

Beautiful ribbon is an elegant final touch for any gift. Here's a decorative finish for the ribbon itself. We learned this trick for making dramatic and perfectly uniform zigzags from Bell'occhio, a wrapping and ribbon emporium in San Francisco.
Fold the end of a ribbon lengthwise an odd number of times. Using pinking or scallop shears, make a cut on the diagonal. Just one fold gives a notch or V-shape; more folds result in zigzags. If necessary, iron the cut ends flat before using.

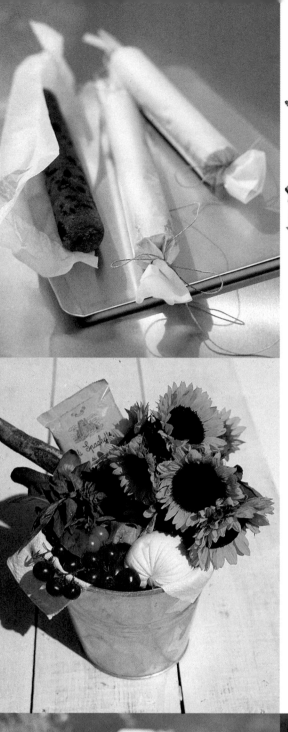

cookie-dough gifts

A sweet way to say thank you is to give your host a batch of homemade cookie dough. Wrap a log of dough in parchment paper and tie the ends with string *(top left)*; refrigerate for a few hours before giving it. But don't tell your host that the dough will keep in the freezer more than a month; he or she might try to postpone baking the cookies until after you leave.

boxed autumn

This autumn, surprise someone with a box full of fall color *(top center)*. Press an assortment of richly hued fallen leaves in a phone book for a few days. Allow them a day or so to curl, then pack and mail them to a friend who lives in a region without fall foliage.

custom bath oils

Spiked with a scent, that old-fashioned home remedy castor oil becomes a luxurious bath oil. Begin by decanting castor oil into clean vintage bottles *(top right)* or into new ones. Add an ounce of essential oil, or blend oils for custom fragrances. Stop bottles with new corks and tag them with hand-drawn or computer-generated labels.

cookie tins

Long after the cookies are gone, these shimmering tins *(middle right)* can be put to good use. Pudding molds, baking pans, and canisters can serve their official culinary purpose, or they can be recycled into flower holders, fruit bowls, or catchalls. Use undyed tissue paper for lining the containers—toxic tints can leach into the cookies.

pie kit

Share your favorite pie—without doing any baking. In a pie pan *(bottom left)*, bundle together essential tools and ingredients, such as fresh fruit, dough wrapped in waxed paper, a rolling pin, and crumb topping; tie with a kitchen towel. Make sure you tuck a written or printed recipe into the package.

for a gardener

When you stock up on perennials in late summer, don't keep them all for yourself. Fill a flat *(bottom center)* with forget-me-nots, lupines, poppies, and hollyhocks, and, when you visit a friend who gardens, give it as a gift.

little luxuries

dinner kit

Next time you're a weekend guest, give your host one less meal to worry about. Line a galvanized-steel pail or a basket with a dish towel, then fill it with everything needed to make dinner *(middle left)*: spaghetti, tomatoes, fresh basil, crusty bread, mozzarella and Parmesan, and flowers for the table.

cup of comfort

When a friend gets a cold or the flu, stop by with a pampering package *(bottom right)*. Fresh gingeroot can be grated and steeped for tea, vintage cotton hankies attend to the sniffles, fresh eucalyptus boiled in a large pot of water makes a sinus-clearing inhaler, honey drops coat a sore throat, and a honey bear sweetens teas.

soap bars

Making soap from scratch is an arduous process, but you can mold these luminous bars by following the instructions on the opposite page. Kitchen supplies and plain, clear soap are all you need to make the colorful bars. Natural additions give soaps a different look and feel; add poppy seeds to melted soap, or a spiral of orange peel between layers. Try other citrus peels, oatmeal, or a fern sprig. Wrap the soaps in parchment paper and tie with twine or slice into little guest bars.

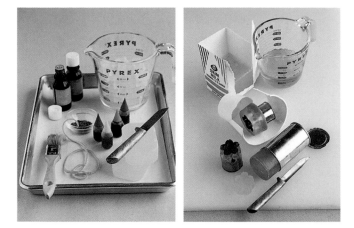

making soap bars

Chop unscented glycerin soap to yield 2 cups of ½-inch chunks. Melt in a double boiler, or microwave on high for about one minute. Skim any froth. Mix in tiny amounts of liquid coloring. If desired, add essential oil for scented soaps. Milk-carton bottoms and smooth-sided tomato-paste cans can be used as molds; the flower soap was molded in a vegetable cutter set in a paper cup. Plastic chocolate molds work well, too. Brush mold with essential oil or vegetable oil; add melted soap; let stand until hardened, about two hours. Rip away carton or cup, or open can bottom; push soap out. For layers, pour soap into mold and let harden for about 20 minutes; skim any bubbles, then add another layer.

making scarves

A handmade scarf is a lovely gift—and simple to make. The four on pegs are made of a quarter-yard of melton wool each; the one over the chair is made from a seven-foot length. For the scarf on the left, hem wool by hand, then iron in half lengthwise. Center ribbon over crease on one side, with ½-inch hem allowance at the end, and pin. Sew along ribbon edges. Repeat on other side. Fold ribbon ends under; stitch down. For the satin-backed scarf, cut wool and satin to size; pin right sides together. Sew with ½-inch seam allowance, leaving 3-inch gap on one side. Trim corners; turn right side out. Iron flat; stitch gap closed. For orange scarf, turn edges ⅛ inch, then ½ inch, then iron flat. Stitch corners down by hand, then blanket-stitch around edge. For velvet-edged scarves, iron 1½-inch-wide velvet ribbon in half lengthwise. A half inch in from edge of wool, sew ribbon to one side; fold ribbon to other. All of these ideas can be adapted to make a scarf of any width or length.

bottle wraps

A bottle of wine is as easy to give as it is to receive, but it's troublesome to wrap in an attractive package. The five ideas here begin with soft, flexible materials that conform to a bottle's contours. Above, from right: A vintage dish towel encloses a country wine. Lay the bottle lengthwise along one side, its bottom 2 inches from the edge. Roll it up and secure with straight pins at 2 inch intervals. Fold the bottom sides inward as you would wrap a box, and pin. Cinch the top with twine. The next bottle is wrapped with two sheets of colored paper, each cut 1 inch wider than half the bottle's circumference, and 7 inches longer than the bottle; scallop the edges with a Fiskars rotary cutter *(left)*. Overlap the sheets by an inch, and tape them together with double-sided tape. Roll

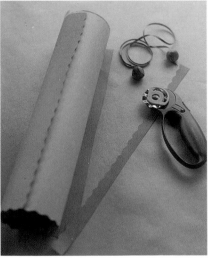

up the bottle, and tape the two remaining edges together. Then fold the bottom under and tape. Center the seam, and flatten the top; fold corners inward. Fold the top down, punch two holes, insert a ribbon, and tie. Finish ribbon ends with a pair of hazelnuts, drilled with a Dremel drill. The other three wrappings begin with several sheets of tissue paper. Lay bottle so that paper extends 2 inches beyond bottom and at least 1 inch beyond top. Before wrapping the bottle, fold paper edges in to create neat outer seams. Roll bottle; secure with double-sided tape beneath the seam. Fold bottom and tape it closed. Fold top over, or cinch it with waxed thread or twine. Finish wrapping with ribbon, twine, pretty paper sleeves, and seasonal details like tiny pinecones or maple leaves.

beaded bookmarks

Lengths of ribbon weighted with buttons and beads mark a page with style, and you can personalize the bookmarks for friends by using alphabet beads and their favorite colors. From left: A big button is sewn to ribbon notched at the end (diagonal cuts prevent grosgrain from unraveling). Ribbon ends are folded into V-shapes and secured with fabric glue, making a sturdy base for the teardrop bead sewn to each end. Two ribbons are sewn together at the button. Knotted silk cord keeps glass and alphabet beads in place. Fancy wide ribbon, folded and glued at the ends, has clear glass beads stitched to top and bottom.

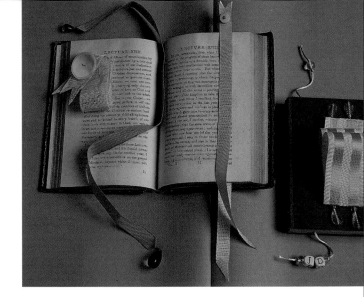

paper clip charms

The classic paper clip was a marvelous invention—but these handmade clips are much more enchanting. They make inexpensive, surprising little gifts, to be used as paper clips or bookmarks; try clipping one onto a homemade card. Use twenty-gauge annealed-iron wire, which bends without chipping or flaking; the best tools are wire cutters and round-nosed pliers used by jewelry makers. Designs can be quite ornate, as long as they consist of at least two flat loops or shapes to slip on either side of a piece of paper. Start with some basic patterns, such as the heart or square. Each requires five inches of wire. To make the heart, begin at the midpoint and bend wire into a right angle; then curl each end around points of pliers, curving the sides into smooth arcs. The letter J is made by wrapping the stem of the J once around the crossbar and twisting it tightly with pliers.

personalized stamps

Produce bookplates, labels, and stationery instantly with a custom-made rubber stamp. Start with a design or message in black ink (drawn by hand or created on the computer) and have a business-supply store or rubber-stamp company create a stamp. Ink pads come in many colors; on vintage books, use archival ink. Spread it on a homemade balsa-wood stamp pad or a piece of glass. Use archival glue to affix bookplates. For other purposes, regular glue works just fine, or you can use adhesive paper and never mess with glue at all.

gardening

[seeds, pots, bouquets, tools]

What could be more satisfying than a successful garden? A handful of seeds is transformed into blooming flowers, leafy plants, and an abundance of fruits and vegetables. Each season brings what seem like miracles, even if you witness them year after year.

The transformation, of course, doesn't occur on its own; as any gardener knows, it is the result of dedication, hard work, and a bit of luck. There aren't too many shortcuts, but there are ways to work more efficiently and effectively. The right tools and techniques will certainly make the time you spend even more enjoyable.

Gardening is a vast topic, so the ideas in this chapter focus on the details. How to make one task easier. How to showcase what you've grown. How to bring the outdoors inside. Spring, summer, autumn, winter, there's always something that needs to be done—and just as often, a way to do it better.

You don't even have to consider yourself a gardener to appreciate all of this information. The front lawn, potted plants, cut flowers waiting to be arranged—they all need your care and attention.

Opposite: A dry gourd can be transformed into a feeder that birds will love. Grow large, bulbous gourds from seed and dry them, or look for them at farm stands. With a 4-inch hole-saw bit, drill a window, then drill four small holes at the top, and loop natural jute through them. Fill partway with birdseed and hang from a tree branch.

twig fence

Often found in English gardens, bent twigs *(top left)* convey the message of a "Keep off the grass" sign, but they look much more natural in their environment and have a lot more charm. Collect flexible twigs to form a fence around freshly seeded patches of grass or any area in the garden where you don't want feet to tread.

storing seeds

Moisture, heat, and fluctuating temperatures are seeds' worst enemies; left out in the shed through the winter, they will lose much of their vigor—the ability to germinate quickly and healthily—and they may even die. Instead of abandoning them to the elements, pamper seeds through the winter. Place them in an airtight container, such as a clean jar with a well-sealed lid *(top center)*. Then make a few moisture-absorbing sachets by wrapping and tying two tablespoons of cat litter (use litter made of clay only, without dyes or fragrance) or powdered milk in a double layer of tulle. Add the sachets to the jars of seed packets, close the lid tightly, and store in a cool, dark place until you're ready to plant the seeds.

keeping roses

Why can't roses last more than a few days in a vase? They can—if you know a few tricks *(middle row)*. First, remove the thorns: Wearing leather work gloves, slide your hand along stem from top to bottom. Remove any foliage from the bottom of the stem. Next, use a sharp knife to cut the stems on a slant, under water if possible. Place the roses into a flask with two inches of warm water (no hotter than 110° degrees) for five minutes; this expedites the flow of water into the stems. Place them in a vase of cool water to which you have added cut-flower food or a teaspoon of sugar and a couple of drops of liquid bleach. The water should reach just below the foliage. To revive wilted flowers, try this: Tie them together, attach an anchor like fishing weights or washers, and submerge them overnight in cool water.

giving seedlings

Any gardener will appreciate a gift of seedlings started in biodegradable pots made of compressed peat moss *(bottom center)*. When the seedlings have sprouted, they can be planted, pots and all, straight into the soil.

gardening tips

a better grip

To get a sure grip on scissors and garden shears, wrap their handles with soft linen-and-cotton twine *(top right)*. Roll five feet of twine into a bundle small enough to fit through the handles. Starting at the base of one handle, secure the free end of the twine with your thumb and loop it around the handle, passing the bundle back through the loop and pulling tight, which creates a half-hitch knot. Continue, aligning the knots to form a herringbone pattern around outer edge.

marking a path

For an entirely different kind of stone path *(bottom right)*, mark a route through the garden with white stones, pebbles, shells, or chunks of marble. After the sun sets, they'll reflect the moonlight, showing you the way.

flowerpot table

A slab of stone and a few flowerpots make a table that blends into the garden so well, it almost looks like something you unearthed while turning the soil. This tabletop is marble, but a piece of slate or even an old wooden door would work just as well. Simply rest the chosen tabletop on four large overturned terra-cotta flowerpots of the same size. Once assembled, the table can be used as a work surface (here, it supports topiaries that are waiting to be trimmed) or as an outdoor coffee table—it's more than sturdy enough to rest your feet on.

garden ramp

A full wheelbarrow tips and sways—and may topple as you navigate it down a garden step. This ramp, covered with chicken wire for traction, makes the going easier.

1. Decide the size you want the ramp to be and cut as many boards as you need to the desired length. Lay them side by side on a flat surface and attach a smaller board as a crosspiece at each end, hammering nails that won't go all the way through the outer boards.

2. Lay the panel on a piece of chicken wire large enough to overlap each side. Wrap the chicken wire around to the back, and secure it with U-hooks. To use the ramp, rest one end on a wide, low piece of wood to make the ramp flush with the step. In the off-season, use it as an outside doormat for scraping muddy boots.

box gardens

Bring spring indoors with tabletop gardens in wooden crates and berry baskets. If crates gape at the corners, pry apart sides, saw boards down, and hammer or staple back together. Line with a piece of a plastic garbage bag (lay down moss or dead leaves first if you don't want it to show through cracks), and poke several nail holes in bottom for drainage; fill with potting soil. Sprinkle generously with grass seed or clover, pat down firmly, and shower with water. Kept in a warm, sunny spot, seeds take ten days to two weeks to sprout. For a flowering garden, add bulbs already in bloom; use a teaspoon to dig holes in the grassy turf, then insert the bulbs. As an alternative, cover the soil with moss instead of planting grass.

tidying a houseplant

Potted plants add life to a room, but the soil they grow in has never done much for any decor. A layer of small round pebbles looks as neat and tidy as a Japanese garden and helps keep the soil moist and shaded, which is just how houseplants like it. Look for small river pebbles at garden shops, and arrange them in concentric circles in your pots.

all-green arrangement

It may be the quintessential color of spring, but somehow green only makes it into bouquets as the incidental stem or leaf. Green deserves its own display. In front is a green hydrangea; behind it is a mix of euphorbias, hydrangeas, and bells of Ireland. Other good green blooms include green tulips, chartreuse gladiola, and lady's mantle. Or you can improvise, using new green buds or leafy branches from your backyard.

hanging bouquets

This old May Day custom is well worth reviving, and it doesn't need to be reserved for the·first of May. Surprise a loved one with a basket hung from his or her doorknob. The baskets themselves can be recycled from household containers *(below)*; fill them with your favorite flowers. Some of the vases can be filled with water; others cannot—take this into consideration when leaving a surprise bouquet.

1. and opposite page. Hammer holes in a tin food can, an antique tin, or other metal container. Thread twine or ribbon through the holes for a handle; knot it on the inside or outside of the tin.

2. Roll a piece of fine-mesh brass screen into a cone shape and secure the seam with straight pins. Add a loop of wire for the handle.

3. Wrap annealed iron wire below the lip of a jelly jar. Loop and twist a second wire around the first one for a handle.

4. Wrap raffia around the top of a mason jar, then tie on more raffia for a handle. Let the lengths of raffia hang naturally.

5. Twist wire into a hook for a tin funnel's handle. Hammer a hole in the funnel, run wire through, and twist to fasten.

6. Knot some sturdy ribbon, cord, or twine around the neck of a hyacinth glass, and leave the ends long enough to loop around the doorknob.

hydrangea wreath

This wreath made from a variety of hydrangeas makes the summer seem to stretch a little further into fall. And if you clip the blossoms at the right moment, the wreath will keep for several years. To make it, you'll need an 18-inch-diameter double-wire wreath frame, 35 feet of 22-gauge wire on a paddle, and fifty to sixty hydrangea clusters in different colors (about twenty branches, depending on size and fullness). Bring in hydrangea branches a few days before they reach their peak; they will continue to age after being cut and may brown if you wait too long. Separate blossom clusters from main branch, leaving 5 to 6 inches of stem; remove leaves. Arrange clusters in loose bouquets of three or four, mixing the colors. Lay a bouquet against the frame, and secure one end of the wire to the frame beneath the stems. Wrap wire around the frame and the stems until secure, about three times. Without clipping wire, place another bouquet against the frame so its blossoms cover the stems of the previous bundle; wrap with wire to secure. Continue adding bouquets and wrapping with wire until the frame is filled. Attach a loop of string or ribbon to the frame to hang the wreath.

grow lamp

Seedlings are eager little things, but they may not get enough light to thrive in the dark days of winter and early spring. With this inexpensive grow lamp made from hardware-store supplies, they'll get all the light they need. You'll need a utility-light kit (which comes with the hood and chains and S-hooks for hanging), two eye-hooks, and two basic fluorescent bulbs: one cool white, one warm white, which will mimic the effect of expensive grow lamps. Install the hood by screwing two eye-hooks into the bottom of a wooden shelf (start the hole with an awl), and hang the lamp to the desired height using the chains and S-hooks. Give the seedlings twelve to fourteen hours of light a day; using a timer makes it easier. Adjust the height of the lamp as the plants grow, keeping the seedlings just a few inches from their source of light.

greenhouse window

Instead of gazing out onto winter's frozen flower beds, turn the window into a mini greenhouse. Herbs, seedlings, and fresh grass will thrive regardless of storms on the other side of the pane. A large, deeply set window that receives lots of light works best. Measure depth and width of frame. Subtract ½ inch from width, and order a piece of ½-inch-thick glass in that size from a glazier; have the edges sanded for a finished look. The shelf supports are strips of molding, available at hardware stores. Cut molding lengths to depth of frame (two per shelf) with a hand saw; sand ends smooth. Using a level and pencil, mark where each support should be, starting at top of frame. Drill three evenly spaced holes just bigger than the head of a wood screw in each support. Holding support against its mark on the window frame, drill starter holes into frame. Attach support to frame, countersinking screws so heads don't show. Repeat with all supports. Fill holes with wood putty, sand them, and paint the supports. Once dry, attach a felt dot or plastic glide to each support end, and rest the glass on top. When it warms up outside, seedlings can be planted, and herbs remain within easy reach.

decorating

[curtains, lamps, finishing touches]

Decorating begins with the broad strokes: the color on the walls, the tiles in the kitchen, the rugs on the floor, the shape of the sofa. All of these components must work together to form a welcoming, useful living space.

But after the basic elements are all in place, there's more to consider. A room's tone can be gently underscored by the details, whether pillows, pictures, or pottery. And the smallest change, like adding pretty edging to a shelf, sometimes makes the most eye-catching alteration.

Most rooms evolve. So don't be afraid to add, subtract, or simply make switches, however minor. If something in a room does not suit your current tastes, fix it; even if your guests don't notice it, you will.

In this chapter, you will find projects for every room in the house. These are the details that will really make a difference. Some require just a few minutes, and none take more than a day to accomplish. Flexible and versatile, most of them can be adapted to any decor. Modify them, trust your own style, follow your own rules. And the best part is that when you do it yourself, the results are precisely what you were looking for.

Opposite: In the kitchen and pantry, shelves are often in plain view, so why not turn them into something special to look at? Shelf edging in shiny tin or crisp white paper can be elegant or playful, simple or intricate, and making it is like cutting paper dolls. Design the edging to complement what's on the shelves.

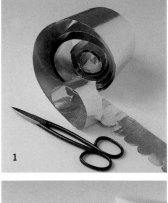

shelf borders

To make the tin shelf border (pictured on page 94), cut a 1½-inch-wide strip of 36-gauge aluminum foil to the length of your shelf using metal snips or scissors; don't use your best scissors, since metal can dull the edges.

1. Cut a scalloped edge along one side of the strip, making evenly spaced arcs 1 inch long. File the cut edge with sandpaper to dull the sharpness. Attach the border to the shelf by hammering flat-head wire nails above each scallop.

2. The white borders *(above)* are made from butcher's paper. First determine the width of the border, based on the shelf's scale and the objects you plan to display. Cut paper strips to that width and the length of your shelf. Fold one strip in half across the width, and repeat folding several times; unfold, and refold accordion-style. Draw a symmetrical pattern and trace half of it on the top of the folded packet, so the folded edge is at the center of the pattern. Cut the shape out through all the layers. For the interior cutouts, a crescent shape was made by folding open the top and bottom flap, then cutting half the crescent through the remaining layers.

3. Unfold the packet to its full length, revealing the pattern. Mount the border along shelf edges with double-sided masking tape or tiny tacks.

cupboard screen doors

Wire mesh is a lot more beautiful and versatile than its common role in window screens would suggest. To replace an old cupboard's broken glass pane or a missing panel with mesh, use metal shears to cut the mesh to 1 inch bigger all around than the space you want to fill. Fold under ⅓ inch on all sides, and staple mesh to the inside of the frame with a staple gun, or attach with tacks. Because wire mesh is available in copper, bronze, aluminum, and stainless steel, you can customize the look to your kitchen.

stacked shelf

This shelf looks good from any angle. Have a lumberyard cut 8 pieces of 1-inch-thick pine board: the largest should be 19½ by 6½ inches; each succeeding one should be 1½ inches shorter and ¾ inch narrower than the one before. Cover one side of the second-largest board with wood glue; attach it to largest. Secure with four 1½-inch finishing nails far enough from edges to be hidden by next board. Continue attaching boards; don't use nails on the last one. Let glue dry, seal shelf with primer, and paint it. Fit the back of shelf with 2 keyhole washers 16 inches apart. Mount shelf on screws set into wall at studs.

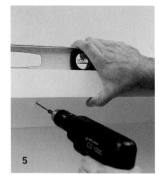

photo display shelf

These narrow picture shelves are a neat, elegant way to display art and photos without making your wall look like a scrapbook. Each shelf requires three pieces of clear pine. The shelf piece itself is ¾ inch by 2½ inches; the support piece is ¼ inch by 4 inches; the lip that keeps pictures in place is ¾ inch by 2 inches; each piece should be as long as you want the shelf to be.

1. Using a miter box to keep the saw square, cut all three pieces to the desired length.

2. Position the lip perpendicular to shelf piece so that it protrudes ¼ inch on one side and 1 inch on other. Join using wood glue and 1½-inch screws at 8-inch intervals. Join support to shelf at right angles in the same way. Countersink screw heads in front.

3. When glue is dry, fill screw sinks with wood putty.

4. Sand and prime wood, then paint with a semigloss enamel.

5. Drill holes through the support piece at 18-inch intervals, as close to the shelf's underside as possible. Use a level to position shelf against wall, then screw shelf to the wall through the holes, countersinking the screw heads. Fill screw sinks with putty; sand and touch up with paint.

lining a cabinet

Give the inside of a cupboard a sense
of surprise with a lining of old maps,
illustrations, sheet music, postcards—
or photocopies of them. This idea can
also work well on open shelving.

   Assemble your artwork. Look for
old documents at flea markets, or buy
a book of reproductions. You can use
the originals, or make black-and-white
photocopies onto colored paper,
enlarging or reducing images to get
the look you want. A proportion
wheel (available at art-supply stores)
helps you calculate the percentage to
enlarge or reduce. Or you can just
improvise, letting a patchwork effect
become part of the charm. The flower
image here is actually numerous pieces
of paper, none exactly aligning, in
various shades of blue.

   Cut papers to fit your cabinet (this
cabinet has pull-out shelving). With a
foam brush, spread on wallpaper paste.
Apply the papers one at a time, and
smooth them with a wooden roller.

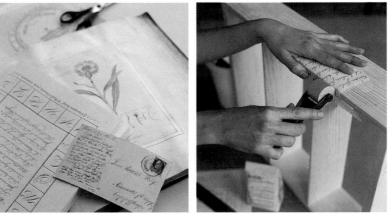

clip frames

An elaborate frame isn't suited to everything you want to display. Two panes of glass show off prints, photos, or pressed plants without a lot of unnecessary expense or fuss. Have a glazier cut two pieces of glass to the desired size, and ask that the edges be honed smooth. Sandwich art between the panels and secure them with stationery-store binder clips.

ornamental hooks

A plaster ornament modeled from a natural or architectural form can hide picture-hanging hardware and also enhance the picture you're hanging. To make the ornaments, knead Super-Elasticlay (a polymer clay available at art-supply stores) until soft and pliable. Coat a small object, such as a shell *(below left)*, a tin architectural mold, or an iron fence decoration, with petroleum jelly or cornstarch. Press object into clay, then remove it and bake the clay at 350° for thirty minutes. As clay mold cools, mix casting plaster (also from art-supply stores) according to instructions on package. Work in small batches; plaster hardens quickly. Coat inside of mold with petroleum jelly or cornstarch. Spoon in wet plaster. Tap mold on work surface to force out bubbles. Let set for a few minutes, then press a molding hook, picture hook, or a piece of bent wire into the back *(below center)*. The molding hook will fit over picture molding; use bent wire if you want to cover an existing nail. Once plaster has dried, gently remove ornament and smooth any rough spots with fine sandpaper. Paint the ornament *(below right)* to match or complement your wall or molding color.

cloverleaf bow

This sturdy bow is pretty enough to serve as a picture hanger. Here's how to make it. Cut three lengths of double-faced satin ribbon in these sizes: one 25-inch length of 4⅝-inch-wide ribbon; one 50-inch length of 4⅝-inch-wide ribbon; one 10-inch length of 1½-inch-wide ribbon. For a contrasting edge, bind wider ribbon with different-color narrow ribbon after measuring.

1. Lay the shorter piece of wide ribbon flat; bring the ends into the center, overlapping slightly.

2. Pleat at center; bind with florist's wire. Find center of longer piece, form a same-size loop, and bind with wire.

3. Iron the narrow ribbon in half lengthwise. Place the short bow across the long one.

4. Crisscross the narrow ribbon around the bow's center.

5. Pull narrow ribbon tight to bind; stitch at the back. Trim ends evenly. To hang art, mount it on the wall using picture wire and a hook. Remove the art; tack ribbon streamers to the frame's back at corners. Rehang; tack bow into wall above frame.

ribbon plate hanger

Suspended from pretty silk ribbon, favorite trays and platters can be on display but still within easy reach. Feed a piece of ribbon (determine the length according to the size of the platter) through a brass ring and sew the ends together securely. Repeat with a second, equal-length ribbon. Hang the ring from a porcelain picture hook and position the seams in the back. Slip a rectangular platter into loops, and let it hang on its own, or add a smaller oval platter in front.

1

2

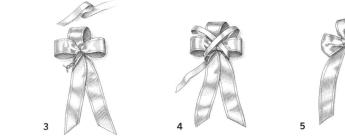

3

4

5

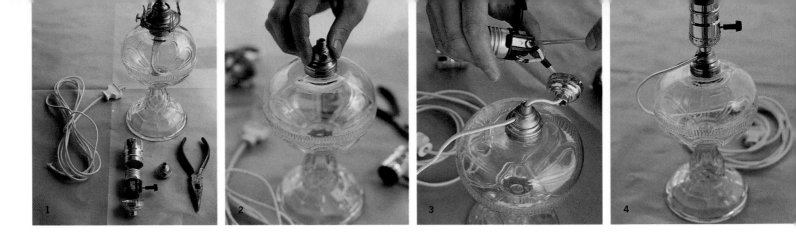

electrified oil lamp

Convert an old oil lamp to electricity, and you can enjoy its glowing light and glass curves without the smoke, smell, and danger of an oil flame. The result *(opposite)* is nineteenth-century design with modern convenience.

1. Unscrew the metal burner, which holds the wick and chimney clamps. Then clean out any residue from the oil reservoir using dishwashing liquid and water. To fit the lamp with a converter, take the old burner to a specialty lighting store. Oil-lamp converters come in three standard sizes that fit most American-made lamps. (If your lamp is missing a burner, you can measure the diameter of the oil-reservoir opening to determine the size you need.) You will also need a lamp socket, a standard lamp cord and plug, and needle-nose pliers.

2. Screw converter into oil reservoir.

3. Pry the metal cap from the lamp socket. Thread the lamp cord into the side hole and out the top hole of the converter, then through the socket cap. Using the pliers, split the end of the cord and remove the rubber insulation from the tips to reveal the wires. Remove the housing of the socket to uncover the screws for the electrical contacts. Wrap each wire end around a contact, and tighten the screws.

4. Screw the socket cap into the converter. Then pull the cord back through the converter until taut, and reassemble the socket. Add desired shade to the finished lamp.

roped table lamp

Coiled around a lamp base, ordinary rope shows off its own natural beauty and texture. Begin with an inexpensive lamp with a large, bulbous base. Purchase 100 feet of three-ply manila (shown here), jute, or sisal rope from a hardware or marine-supply store. Before attaching it, coil it around the base to make sure it's long enough. Starting at the bottom, use a ¾-inch bright brush (which has a flat, compact head) to apply heavy-duty all-purpose glue, such as Weldbond, to the lamp base in 6-inch sections. Begin wrapping the rope around the base, holding it in place until the glue begins to set, 10 to 20 seconds. Press each layer snug against the one below it, making sure there are no gaps. Trim the end on an angle and tuck it beneath the previous coil. Top off the lamp with a natural-colored shade made of linen or parchment.

painting lampshades

The right lampshade can transform a room, but first you have find it. Here's how to make the shade that you want. Start with an opaque white paper shade, available at housewares and lighting stores, in the desired size. Then customize it with paint, trim, or silver leaf to complement the base and the room the lamp will illuminate.

High-gloss oil-base paint gives best results. Thin the paint if necessary, and apply two or three coats to the outside of the shade, letting it dry thoroughly after each coat. This may be all the embellishment the shade needs *(far right)*.

For a more finished look, add ribbon trim *(middle right)*. Cut two pieces of ribbon; one should be equal to the circumference of the shade's top, the other to the bottom. Paint the top edge of the shade with craft glue, and lay the ribbon over the glue with the ends meeting at the shade's seam. Repeat for the bottom edge.

The wide silver trim *(near right)* is self-adhesive but stiff, so it can only be used on a drum-shape shade; it was scoured gently with steel wool to give it a matte look.

A lining of silver leaf gives lamplight a gentle glow. It should be applied before you paint the shade. Use a paintbrush to spread a thin coat of gilder's adhesive, or size, to the inside of the shade. Pick up a sheet of silver leaf with a static brush *(above)* to transfer it to the shade (avoid touching the silver leaf with your hands; fingerprints

could tarnish it). Continue adding sheets of silver leaf, one at a time, starting at the bottom and overlapping them slightly, until the interior of the shade is entirely covered. Use a clean, soft cloth to rub the silver leaf gently, removing bits that didn't adhere *(right)*. It's a good idea to coat the silver leaf with a clear acrylic sealer to help prevent tarnishing.

vintage shutter doors

With their clean lines and handcrafted details, the old wooden shutters found at flea markets and secondhand shops can be put to good use indoors. Their long shape is often ideal for the doorway of a narrow closet or the front of a cabinet. This shutter with the evergreen cutout was painted white and attached to a hall cupboard; vintage hinges and knob make a fitting finish.

dish-towel curtains

Made from vintage linen dish towels, these casual curtains are the perfect cover-up for windows in a kitchen or a bare summer rental. You'll need two dish towels, two cup hooks, a length of bamboo, and café clips. Screw a cup hook on either front side of the window frame, halfway up; if necessary, start the holes with a nail. Saw the bamboo to a length that extends from one hook to the other, with a bit of overhang on each end. Thread the clip rings onto the bamboo, rest the bamboo over the hooks, and clip both of the dish towels in place.

tea-towel bistro curtains

The classic café curtain hangs across the lower half of a window, providing a bit of privacy without restricting sunshine. This version, made with a large vintage tea towel, achieves the same romantic effect with very little sewing. You'll need a curtain rod (brass, if you want the traditional bistro look) and matching sew-on rings. Cut the towel across its width and turn the top half around so the towel's ends become the bottom borders of each curtain. Measure the window from the sill to where you want the rod to hang, then hem the top end of each curtain to that measurement. Stitch the rings to the curtain, install the rod, and hang the curtain from it.

trimming pillowcases

Instead of banishing odd lengths of beautiful fabric or lace to the ragbag, use them to embellish the hems of plain pillowcases. Start with crisp white cases, and sew on a variety of trimmings that complement the rest of the bed linens. Monogrammed handkerchiefs, often found at flea markets, can be folded diagonally and machine-stitched to a case, creating a wonderful present for someone with the right initial.

covering a box spring

As its name implies, a dust ruffle is often frilly. But if you use a top sheet, tablecloth, or any plain fabric instead, it will be as crisp and tailored as the rest of the bedding. If using a sheet, it should should be the same size as the bed: a twin for a twin bed, a queen for a queen. If using a tablecloth or other fabric, determine the width by doubling the height of the box spring and adding its width plus six inches. Calculate the length by doubling the box spring's height, then adding its length plus six inches. After you've sewn a one-inch hem all the way around, this will result in a rectangle of fabric that covers the box spring and hangs down an extra two inches on all sides.

Don't pass up a good wooden chair just because the seat cushion is tattered; recover the seat yourself. Begin by removing the cover and padding until you hit the center board. If it is damaged, trace it onto a piece of ¼-inch-thick plywood. Cut out the new seat board with a jigsaw or have it done at a lumberyard.

1. Trace the board onto 1-inch-thick foam, then cut the foam so it's ⅛ inch larger than the outline. Place the board on the foam. Cut batting fabric 4 inches larger than the board. Place the board and foam on batting. Pull one side of the batting over the board and staple it 1½ inches from the edge. Pull the opposite side tight and staple. Staple remaining sides.

2. Cut a piece of upholstery fabric 4 inches larger than the seat, then staple it as you did the batting.

3. To cover the rough underside, cut a piece of lining fabric 2 inches smaller than the seat, and staple it all around the underside. Reattach the finished seat to the chair.

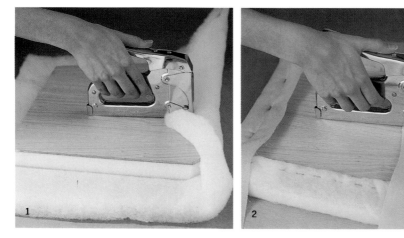

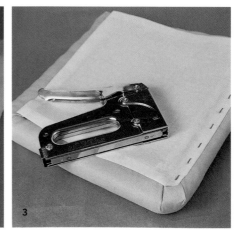

fabric tabletop

If the surface of a favorite table or desk is showing signs of wear, don't give up on it—extend its life with a covering of canvas, linen, or leather.

Start by measuring the tabletop's width, length, and thickness. Double the thickness and add this number to all sides; cut a piece of durable fabric or leather to this size. Along each edge, fold a hem equal to the thickness of the table and iron flat.

Using a hammer covered with cloth, secure the fabric to one side of the tabletop with upholstery tacks at 1½-inch intervals; begin at one corner and complete the entire side. Then stretch the fabric across the surface of the table and secure it with more upholstery tacks at the remaining corners, folding fabric under to make a vertical seam at each corner. Finish by tacking the three remaining sides the same way as the first.

Of course, you don't have to wait until a tabletop is scratched or worn to employ this technique; it can be used to give any table a fresh look.

storage cubes

A medicine cabinet is never roomy enough for all the bathroom necessities. These cubbyholes add just the right amount of storage. Their manageable size also keeps the contents neat and organized. A single box might be enough, or you can create a column, row, or grid of identical cubes.

Each of the boxes is made from five pieces of ¾-inch-thick plywood; the sides are 12 inches long by 9 inches wide; the back is 12 inches square. The four sides are mitered along the ends, glued together, and secured with 1½-inch finishing nails. Or, instead of doing the mitering, you can have the lumberyard cut the boards for the box's top and bottom 10½ inches long by 9 inches wide, and the sides 12 by 9 inches. Glue the ends of the bottom and top boards to the inside edges of the side boards; secure with finishing nails. Glue on the back and secure with more nails. Sand any rough spots smooth, apply a primer, and paint the wood. The finished boxes can be screwed right into the wall through their back panels (center them on a stud). Countersink the screw heads, putty them, and touch up with paint.

towel ladder

After a few trips to the beach or pool, is every rack, hook, and railing in the house draped with damp towels? The rungs of a progressive or apple-picking ladder supply the extra hanging spots you need. Prop it against a bathroom wall or corner, or on the porch so sand doesn't find its way indoors. To keep the ladder from slipping, attach the rubber tips made for chair legs to its feet. For added stability, you can use a hook and eye to fasten it to the wall.

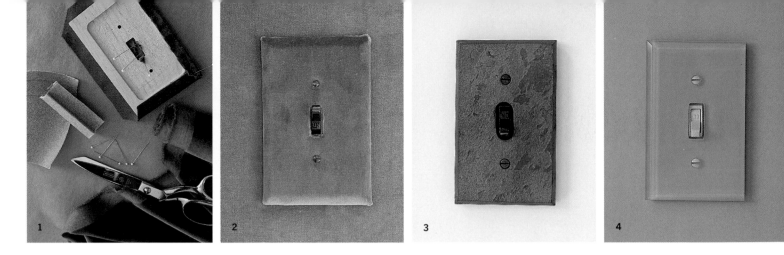

custom switch plates

Switch plates are to a room what buttons are to clothing: With a little effort, you can make them one of a room's nicest details.
1. and **2**. To cover a wooden switch plate in velvet, or any other fabric, first sand the inside of the rectangular hole to enlarge it a bit. Cut velvet to ⅜ inch larger than the plate; trim corners as shown. Apply glue to the four edges of the velvet and pin down. Use a utility knife to cut an X in the velvet covering the hole for the switch; fold back the resulting triangles of velvet, glue them in place, and pin. Remove pins when glue is dry. With an awl, make holes in velvet through screwholes.
3. For a slate switch plate, have a stonemason cut one from roofing tile; provide a standard plate to use as a model.
4. A glass switch plate can be painted to match any room. Order a switch plate with polished edges from a glazier, and paint the back of the plate with flat wall paint to match or complement the wall.

homemade tole

Tole, the eighteenth-century painted tinware that is prized today by collectors, provided the inspiration for these colorful buckets. They mimic the look for a fraction of the price. Use them as wastebaskets, vases, or catchalls. Each one starts as a plain tin or galvanized-aluminum bucket.

To make the bucket with dots around the rim *(near right)*, begin by painting a 3-inch stripe in yellow paint around the top of the bucket, and let it dry. Place 1-inch-diameter round adhesive stickers along the strip at equal intervals. Paint the entire outside of the bucket brick-red, taking care not to get any paint under the stickers. Let the paint dry, then peel off the stickers, allowing the yellow dots to show through.

For the banded bucket *(far right)*, start by painting a bucket rust red. Secure a ½-inch-wide band of drafting tape around the bucket about two-thirds of the way down. Paint the area above the tape yellow. Let the paint dry, then remove the tape. Place strips of tape above and below where the yellow meets the red, leaving a ½-inch gap between them. Paint the gap beige, let paint dry, and peel off the tape.

For the harlequin bucket *(below center),* start by painting the bucket off-white. Then use overlapping strips of drafting tape to form the triangle pattern, trimming the tape with an X-Acto knife as necessary to acheive the points. Paint the area inside the resulting triangles blue.

Each of these designs can be adapted and modified; create new patterns and use your favorite colors.

homekeeping

Houses are busy places. Cooking, gardening, crafts, homework, paperwork, cleaning up—it's all more manageable and enjoyable if you're organized.

To keep things running efficiently, think about how you use the tools and supplies throughout your house, and arrange them accordingly. Tackle one area at a time. Instead of overhauling the kitchen, make sense of just the pots and pans. Open up the drawer that acts as a catchall for all those odds and ends (every house has one) and empty it. Find a logical place for whatever's worth keeping, and be ruthless about discarding the rest.

Make a list of the things you've been meaning to buy, whether pinking shears, a better mop, or new computer software, and buy them now. But be selective; know the difference between a purchase that saves time or makes you more creative and one that adds to the clutter.

You don't need limitless space to be productive. Gain more storage with stackable plastic bins and portable tool chests. Scan flea markets for attractive old baskets, boxes, and cabinets. And always keep in mind that even if something's purpose is practical, it should still look good.

Opposite: At last, a bulletin board that you won't want to hide on the back of a closet door. In place of a drab expanse of cork, overlapping layers of ribbon provide pockets for notes, invitations, and receipts; photos stay flat and free from tack holes. But don't cover it completely with mementos; the board itself is worth showing off.

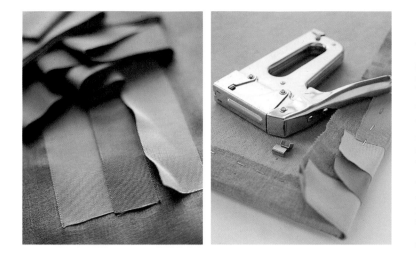

ribbon bulletin board

The ribbon board on page 112 is made from grosgrain ribbons sewn onto a piece of linen, which is attached to Homosote, a compressed-paper board. Start with a 25-by-34-inch piece of linen. Choose ribbons in widths from 1½ to 6 inches; trim to 25-inch lengths. Lay a wide ribbon along one short side of the linen 3 inches from edge; this will be the top border. Sew it down along top and bottom edges. Place the next ribbon so it just overlaps bottom seam of first; sew along its bottom edge. Continue adding ribbons until linen is covered. Stretch fabric around a 21-by-30-inch Homosote board, and secure to the back using a staple gun. Attach picture hangers to back, and hang.

ribbon rack

If spools of ribbon are threatening to take over your craft area, give them some space of their own. They'll stay accessible and untangled in storage racks fashioned from copper gutters—and the ribbons will even add a decorative element to your workspace. Measure the available wall space, then have a lumberyard cut a half-round gutter to the length you need and cap the ends. Punch several holes along top edge and mount in a dry place away from direct sunlight, which will fade ribbons.

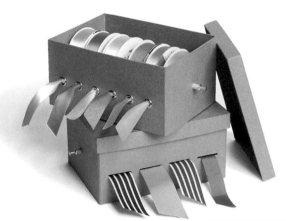

ribbon box

Here's another way to keep ribbons organized and tangle-free. Start with a cardboard box (a shoebox will do). To install grommets for dispensers, make round holes with a utility knife. Push male half of grommet through hole and rest on anvil; add female half, set mandrel in place, and hammer. (Or, instead of grommets, make slits for the dispensers.) Make a ¼-inch round hole on box ends. Trim a ¼-inch dowel so it's just longer than box. Place spools inside; slide dowel through the box and spools. Pushpins on dowel ends keep it in place.

homemade notebooks

Stray thoughts seem to take on new significance when they're written in a handcrafted notebook. Any paper can be used for pages; cut it to size yourself, or buy notepaper in office-supply stores. For front and back covers, use stiff paper, either two separate pieces or one wraparound piece; the buff-colored notebook at top doesn't have a cover at all.

1. Use a bone folder, a simple tool that creases without cutting, to make a crease in the cover so it opens easily.

2. Make holes with an awl, or use a hole punch, which does a cleaner job but only goes through a few sheets at a time. Start with a template for a single sheet of paper, and use it to make holes that line up.

3. For the "garden notes" book, make two holes; from the back, poke the ends of a rubber band through the holes, then secure by threading a twig (or pencil, skewer, or other long, thin object) through rubber-band loops.

4. Use an upholstery needle to stitch pages together. For simple stitches and larger holes, thread string through by hand (see the blue book with white twill tape and yellow one with black ribbon); just tie it off tightly in back. The pink notebook is bound with black waxed twine in a buttonhole stitch: Starting at the top or bottom, stitch through each hole from front to back; when the needle comes out the back, send it though the loop of thread before pulling it tight.

key cabinet

A busy house can feel like a hotel, so why not borrow an idea from innkeepers and hang everyone's keys in a box? This box *(top left)* came in unfinished pine; it was painted white and given a porcelain handle. An old medicine chest or cigar box can do the trick, too. Just screw the desired number of cup hooks on the inside.

seed-packet file

Seed packets have a funny way of disappearing, then turning up at the bottom of a drawer after you've ordered more. Keep track of them in a wicker-basket file *(top center)* organized with index cards and divider tabs. Once a packet is open, transfer remaining seeds to a coin envelope, clipping the original packet to it. Keep file in a cool, dry place.

medicine-chest makeover

If opening your bathroom cabinet invites an avalanche of cotton balls, try a new kind of cleansing ritual: Reorganize the medicine chest. Found objects and flea-market bargains make appealing, tidy keepers for toiletries *(top right)*. Cotton balls fill a vintage

twine hangers

To keep balls of string from tangling or unraveling, try this solution. Hang spools of twine and cord on knotted ribbons *(middle left)*. Turn the ribbons' knots so they are hidden inside the rolls of string. Then suspend from hooks screwed into a wall in your work area.

warranty file

A broken appliance is always annoying, but if you've lost the warranty or manual, it's positively maddening. Keep all those papers and guides in an accordion file *(middle center)*, categorized with handwritten labels.

covered crocks

Trash may be an unavoidable part of life, but an unsightly container isn't. We found these vintage pickling crocks *(middle right)* in various sizes at antiques stores and flea markets. A roofer made aluminum lids with handles (to get the correct lid size, measure the crock's circumference on the outside and add one inch). Use the covered crocks to store garbage, recyclables, or dry dog food.

organizing tips

teacup, and bobby pins are perched in an eggcup. Sprinkle talcum powder from a tin sugar shaker, and swig mouthwash from an old flask. Don't forget to clean containers thoroughly, and clearly label any obscure items.

roller towel

With this useful old-house idea *(bottom center and right)*, a hand towel is always within arm's reach in the kitchen or bathroom. Simply stitch two linen hand towels together at both ends to form a loop. Paint a ½-inch wooden dowel in white enamel, and screw porcelain drawer knobs into each end. Slip the towel loop over the dowel, and hang from two wall hooks.

first-aid kit

Like a good insurance policy, a first-aid kit can take away some of life's anxiety. Don't wait until you need it—stock a versatile first-aid kit now. Everything you need can be found at a good drug store. Ready-made kits are widely available, but if you assemble your own, you can tailor it to your needs. For example, you'll want to include a bottle of calamine lotion if you're apt to stumble across poison ivy while bird-watching.

The American Red Cross lists the following as essentials for any kit: adhesive bandages in assorted sizes, sterile gauze rolls or pads, adhesive tape, scissors, tweezers, elastic bandages, a chemical cold pack, antiseptic wipes, aspirin and acetaminophen, ipecac syrup (to induce vomiting), antibiotic cream, and activated-charcoal solution (to absorb caustic poisons).

Pack all of the supplies into a carrying case, such as an old lunch box or small tool chest, and label the case clearly as a first-aid kit. Keep it someplace accessible—but out of reach of small children—and make sure everyone in the house knows where to find it and how to use everything in it.

sewing box

A smart sewing kit doesn't contain every gadget imaginable; it's tailored to meet your wardrobe's needs. Basics include all-purpose thread in colors to match your clothes and needles in assorted sizes. Add a variety of notions, such as snaps, hooks and eyes, seam binding, elastic, iron-on tape or patches, straight pins, safety pins, a needle threader, a tape measure, and a thimble. It's also a good idea to include a pair of scissors, a seam ripper, and a pincushion. A cigar box is just the right size for these essentials; it's shallow enough that you can find all of its contents without having to rummage through them. Glue edges of a length of wide grosgrain ribbon to the inside of the lid for storing needles and easy-to-lose buttons.

organizing a car

A vehicle can come to feel like a second home. To make it safe and comfortable, replace the clutter with a few well-chosen objects.

1. Safety gear stays neat and accessible in a clear plastic box.

2. In the car-door pocket, maps and a cellular phone are within easy reach.

3. A tote bag with cups, plates, and paper towels keeps you prepared for picnics while traveling.

4. A cosmetics kit makes long rides more enjoyable; stock it with aspirin, moisturizer, a nail file, tissues, a comb, lip balm, and adhesive bandages.

5. Every car should have basic safety equipment: jumper cables, flashlight and fresh batteries, tire jack, flare or reflector triangle, first-aid kit, fire extinguisher, windshield-washer fluid, and work gloves. In cold climates, add an ice scraper and snow brush, small shovel, sand or nonclumping cat litter, spray de-icer, blanket, and an empty coffee can and candle, for heat.

6. The glove compartment is the ideal place for small essentials, such as the owner's manual, car registration or a copy of it, repair log, and sunglasses; add a disposable camera to capture memorable moments on the road.

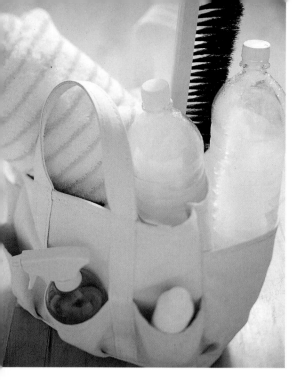

beach caddy

A day at the beach is a breeze if you're well equipped. Convert a canvas tool bag into a tote. Inside, place plastic bottles that have been filled nearly to the top with water and have been frozen; as ice melts, you'll have a constant supply of cool water. Fill a plastic spray bottle with distilled water mixed with a few drops of chamomile oil to mist over parched skin. Use a soft-bristled brush to whisk sand off your feet at the car.

wire-basket shelf

This convenient shelf provides storage in a tight spot. Begin with a wire letter basket. For shelf size, add ½ inch to width of basket's rim and subtract ¼ inch from depth; ask a glazier to cut two panes of Plexiglas or glass to these measurements. Use 2-inch nails to attach the basket to the wall in a bathroom, kitchen, or work area; slide shelves into place.

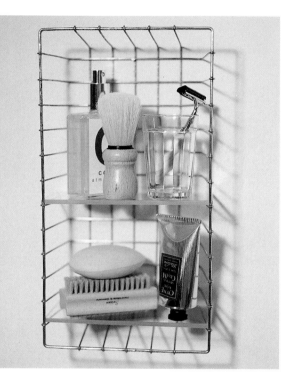

picnic kit

A loaf of bread, a jug of wine, and thou: It may sound like the perfect picnic, but couldn't you use cups to hold the wine and a knife to slice the bread? Be prepared for outdoor feasts with this permanent picnic kit. In a lidded box or basket, pack such things as enamel plates, metal cups, flatware, serving spoons, a pocket knife, and a corkscrew. Add nonperishables like salt, pepper, and sugar, along with napkins, moist towelettes, matches, and votive candles. Dog collars (new, of course) help bundle small items together so they stay in place; a belt secures the entire kit. Store it in your car's trunk or pack it in your suitcase when you travel.

hanging-basket bins

If it seems that there's never enough storage in the kitchen, put baskets to good use. Wicker (or wire) bicycle baskets or fishermen's tackle baskets are sturdy, attractive, and come ready-made with two holes in the back. Hang them on a kitchen wall with cup hooks or on a peg board with peg-board hooks. They make great receptacles for those unwieldy utensils you reach for often, such as whisks and rolling pins, and fruits and vegetables that shouldn't be refrigerated.

button magnets

Part bulletin board, part scrap book, the outside of the refrigerator can get as cluttered as the inside. Give it a unified look with simple, unfussy magnets made from buttons. Look through your stash for charming or unusual old buttons, or peruse garage sales and flea markets for them. Hot glue each one to a small magnet, and it's ready for the fridge.

string pouch

Does that ball of string look like the cat's been batting it around? Make a holder to keep it neat. Cut two pieces of fabric to desired size plus seam allowance. Add an eyelet in one half for the dispenser. With right sides together, sew along sides and bottom of the fabric, forming a bag. Add more eyelets to suspend the bag from hooks, or a twill-tape handle to hang it from a doorknob.

making binders

Create your own cookbooks by keeping recipes in binders. Slip wallpaper scraps or gift wrap into the clear plastic covers of three-ring binders *(top left)*, and label each one accordingly. The illustrations on labels were found in a clip-art book (available at bookstores); paste or photocopy them onto the labels. Use separate binders for different categories or courses; for smaller collections, use dividers within the binder. Keep recipes in a folder pocket or envelopes punched with holes until you're ready to paste them onto heavy-paper pages *(top center)*. As an alternative to adhesive labels, snap binder clips *(top right)* onto the spines of your books.

filing in folders

Stop clipping recipes and tucking them away where you'll never find them. As soon as a recipe catches your eye, drop it into an accordion folder organized with tabs and handwritten labels *(middle left)*. Look for folders in colors that complement your kitchen.

boxes and gifts

Don't forget the classic recipe box; it's still ideal for a collection of recipe cards *(middle right)*. The cards, filled with your favorite recipes, also make excellent gifts. Write or print them out onto the cards, then present them in a special way. Wrap them with ribbon and use a dried leaf as a tag. Cut a strip of art paper long enough so the ends overlap when wrapped around the cards. Cut the ends into semicircles. At one end where the curve of the semicircle begins, make a cut halfway from the bottom to the top of the strip. At the other end, make a cut halfway from the top to the bottom. Wrap the strip around the card and hook together at the two cuts. The knife, fork, spoon, and plate were made with rubber stamps.

organizing recipes

computerizing the kitchen

The computer is a valuable kitchen gadget. Recipes can be typed in, or you can use a recipe software program, which may also help you create menus and shopping lists. Print the recipes out onto card stock *(middle center)*, cut to size, and keep them in plastic binder envelopes. Computer paper also comes in a recipe-friendly size, with pre-punched holes. Keep the disks handy in plastic sleeves in the binder.

laminating cards

Shielded from inevitable spills and splashes, recipes last longer. Purchase self-stick laminating paper at office-supply stores; cut it about an inch larger than the recipe card or paper you want to encase. Peel off backing and stick one piece to front of recipe, another to back. Trim excess lamination *(bottom center and right)*, leaving about ¼ inch all around.

Eucalyptus has long been known for its sinus-clearing aroma. In Australia, where the gum tree grows, brews of its green, leathery leaves are kept simmering on the stove at the first sign of a sore throat. A sprig of fresh eucalyptus (available at many floral shops), hung in the shower, will wake you up and brace you for another day.

soap bottles

In an attractive glass bottle, dishwashing liquid doesn't have to hide beneath the sink. Decorative bottles are available at housewares stores, or you can use a vintage one; just make sure it's perfectly clean. Fill the bottle with dishwashing liquid, and top it with a pour spout (also found at housewares stores). It makes economical and ecological sense, too: You can buy soap in quantity and refill as needed, throwing away less packaging.

nonslip board

A cutting board that slides across the counter as you work isn't just inconvenient, it's also dangerous. The same nonslip mesh that keeps a rug from slipping under your feet will also keep cutting boards in place. Available from housewares stores, it will steady mixing bowls as well.

dish-towel apron

They're cheery, easy to clean, and inexpensive—of course dish towels make the perfect apron. You'll need two towels. The first, placed vertically, serves as bib and back of apron's pockets. The second wraps around wearer's hips and provides outside of pockets. Fold and hem long sides of first towel to desired width. Next, hem bottom of this towel to desired pocket depth. Lay second towel across first, horizontally, leaving 4 inches of overhang at base; sew towels together along bottom and side edges. Stitch a line vertically up center. To create ties for around the neck, cut two 12-inch lengths of ¾-inch twill tape; stitch one end of each to top of bib. Repeat for waist ties, but cut them longer: 14 inches apiece for the average waist.

creasing tablecloths

Master still-life painters had an eye for household detail: the perfect jug, the prized candlestick, the creased tablecloth. Instead of obliterating its folds, enjoy the old-world elegance of a tablecloth with creases. Just any crease won't do, however. After washing a linen tablecloth, iron flat and spray with sizing. Fold carefully into a square, cover with a towel, and either iron in the creases or store weighted with heavy books. For dry-cleaned linens, leave in cleaner's crease; iron a second line along width of cloth. Unfolded, the tablecloth adds a striking geometry to any table.

ironing monograms

Embroidered monograms look best when they pop up crisply from the polished linen around them. To keep them looking sharp and distinct, lay the monogram face down on a towel, and iron it from behind. Remove the towel, and iron around the monogram from the front; avoid ironing directly over the embroidered design.

velvet shoe bags

These little velvet sacks protect shoes from the closet's clutter and are perfect for traveling. Dividing the bag into two pockets prevents shoes from knocking into each other. Cut a 13-by-36-inch rectangle of thick, soft velvet. Fold it in half, right sides facing, and sew up the sides, leaving open a 1-inch gap on each side, about 5 inches from top. Fold top of bag down beyond the holes to create a 3½-inch hem. Pin in place; sew two seams across the bag on each side of holes to form a drawstring casing. Sew a seam up middle of bag to casing. Cut two 40-inch-long pieces of cord for drawstring; put a safety pin at end of strings; run each cord one and a half times through casing. When finished, knot ends and fray to create tassels.

hot-water-bottle case

A freshly filled hot-water bottle can be too hot to handle; this homemade case makes the perfect buffer. Cut two rectangles of fabric about 2 inches wider and longer than the body of the hot-water bottle when full. With right sides of fabric facing, sew one side and bottom together, then sew other side, leaving an opening an inch from the top for the drawstring. Hem the top with a 1-inch seam, and thread cord or ribbon through. Slip cover over your hot-water bottle, cinch, and tie cord—and slip into bed.

striped door snake

Don't let drafts slip in or the heat slip out; block the bit of space beneath the door with a fabric snake weighted with beans. Cut strips of fabric 4½ inches wide in two complementary colors (length depends on how wide you want the stripes). Stitch the strips together along their width until the resulting striped rectangle is about two inches longer than the drafty door frame or windowsill. To make the tube, fold the fabric in half lengthwise, right side facing in; machine-stitch side seam, leaving a three-inch opening at the center of the snake. Stitch each end shut. Turn the snake right side out, fill it with dried navy beans or black-eyed peas, and hand-stitch the opening shut. Wedge the finished snake at the base of the door or window.

removable clothesline

Take advantage of warm, breezy days by drying clothes the old-fashioned way. Line drying is remarkably effective and energy-efficient—and that clean, fresh smell is worth the extra effort. This removable clothesline can be kept coiled on the porch and rigged up in seconds. Buy a clothesline long enough to span the distance between a porch and a nearby tree or post. On the porch end, thread the line through a metal eye hook and wind around a sailor's cleat installed about a foot below the eye. At the other end, screw a hook into the tree or post. Tie the clothesline to a snap shackle, which attaches to the hook.

tools & materials

[craft essentials, special supplies]

Any job is easier with the right tools. This glossary explains many of those you need for the projects in this book; each deserves a spot in any well-stocked craft kit. Organize supplies in toolboxes, drawers, or plastic bins, and make a convenient place for them near your work area, whether it's a family room, kitchen table, basement, or laundry room. Always buy good-quality tools and supplies—you will use them again and again.

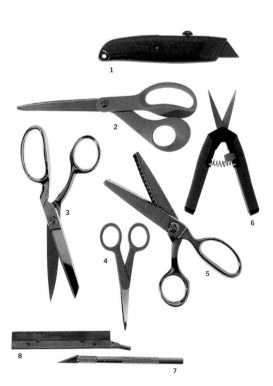

SCISSORS AND BLADES

1. Retractable utility knife With its chunky handle, this useful knife is easy to hold. The blade retracts into the handle for safety. Use it to cut cardboard and other heavy paper and craft materials.

2. and 3. Sewing shears Both of these are bent-handled sewing shears; this means that the blades are slightly angled, allowing you to cut fabric as it lies on a flat work surface. The plastic-handled pair is comfortable and lightweight; forged-steel scissors are well worth the investment for anyone who does a lot of sewing. Never use fabric shears on paper; it will dull the blades. Have a separate pair of paper scissors, and tie tags onto the handles to remind yourself and borrowers which pair is which.

4. Small scissors Lightweight and convenient, these are good for clipping threads or for other small cutting jobs.

5. Pinking shears A zigzag cutting edge distinguishes these from other shears. Useful for fabric, they help keep a raw edge from unraveling. With paper and other craft materials, they're good for decorative edging. Always use separate pairs for fabric and paper. Scallop shears create a scalloped edge.

6. Pointed trimmers These specialty scissors come in handy for many jobs. The thin, pointed tip allows you to reach tight spots; the cushioned handles are easy on the hands.

7. and 8. X-Acto knife and saw blade The thin handle and sharp, pointed blade offer precision for detail cutting. An X-Acto knife and a utility knife are interchangeable for many jobs; the choice is a matter of your preference. A variety of blades are available; use this saw blade to cut thin wooden dowels, for example.

TAPES AND GLUES

1. Floral tape A necessity for making decorations with dried or fresh flowers, floral tape sticks only to itself, so it must be wrapped in tight overlapping layers to adhere. Use floral tape to wrap wire stems, or to bind several stems together; its slightly waxy finish allows it to sit in water. Available in white or green.

2. Gloss medium When mixed in, gloss medium gives paint a shinier, sheerer look. It also acts as an adhesive and gloss varnish, making it useful for découpage and other paper projects.

3. Glue gun The ultimate craft tool. Insert glue sticks into the gun; when heated, the end of the stick melts; pressure on the trigger releases the glue. The glue is thick so it doesn't drip, and it dries quickly. Look for a model that operates at a low temperature or has a low-temperature setting, making it safer for both the user and any delicate materials.

4. Wood glue This glue penetrates wood for a stronger bond. Use to attach wood pieces before nailing together.

5. Craft and fabric glue This ideal all-purpose glue dries clear. Use on paper, fabric, wood, leather, and any other porous materials. Dispense the glue with the squeeze-top, or pour some into a small dish and use a paint brush to coat large surfaces evenly.

6. White artist's tape Most pens will write on this opaque tape; it is also easy to remove from many surfaces.

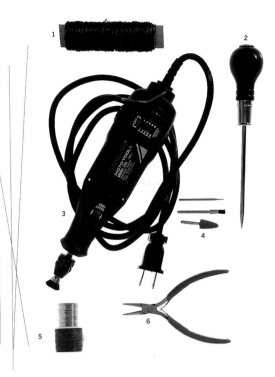

CUTTERS AND FASTENERS

1. Gardening shears A good pair of gardening shears is useful indoors as well as out. Use them to trim woody flower stems before arranging. Look for a spring-action pair with a notch in the blades for clipping wires.

2. and 3. Rotary cutters Like a pizza wheel, this cutter creates a smooth, continuous cut as it rotates. Choose from several wheels, which offer a variety of decorative edges, such as a wavy edge or pinked edge. Use with paper or other craft materials.

4. Staple gun For attaching fabric to wood and for other tacking jobs, a staple gun is indispensable.

5. Wire cutters Short, straight blades snip wires easily. When working with metal, look for jewelers' tools at craft stores.

6. Metal snips Use these for cutting sheet metal or heavy-duty aluminum foil. They cut metal smoothly without crimping or bending it.

7. Hole punch Use it for decoration or gift tags. The standard office-supply size is ¼ inch; for crafts, also look for ⅛ inch. Other shapes, such as diamonds, hearts, and squares, are also available.

WIRES AND MISCELLANEOUS TOOLS

1. Floral wire Use flexible, sturdy, plastic-coated floral wire to secure stems to other objects, such as a wreath form. When making bouquets, flowers with thick stems are often given new stems of this thin wire. A small paddle is particularly easy to handle.

2. Awl A simple tool used to pierce holes in leather, stacks of paper, thin metal sheeting, and other materials.

3. and 4. Dremel rotary tool and bits The convenient size and versatility of this hand-held tool makes it excellent for craft projects. A wide selection of bits allows it to drill, cut, grind, sharpen, buff, and polish.

5. Wires Keep a supply of wires on hand for different projects. The top spool is 22-gauge aluminum wire, below it is 20-gauge annealed iron wire, and to the left are precut lengths of brass wire. The smaller the gauge, the thicker the wire.

6. Round-nose pliers Useful for jewelry-making and other wire work, these shears easily twist wire into small loops, without crimping or scratching it.

MISCELLANEOUS TOOLS

1. Ruler No work area should be without a standard ruler; this one has a cork back to keep it from slipping. A flexible, retractable measuring tape is another necessity.

2. Self-healing cutting mat Protect your work surface with a mat when using cutting tools. Cuts virtually disappear from this mat, leaving a smooth surface. The grid pattern also helps you line up your materials.

3. and 4. Grommet tools and grommets Grommets are like heavy-duty eyelets, used for fabrics such as canvas and leather. Each one has a male and female half. To install one, you'll need a grommet kit, which includes the hole-making tool, anvil, and mandrel. Begin by making a hole in the fabric with the appropriate tool. Place the male half of the grommet on the anvil; lay the fabric on top so the protruding ring on the grommet is inserted through the hole. Add the female half, set the mandrel in place, and hammer.

5. Eyelets These two-part metal reinforcements are for holes in fabric. Look for eyelet kits in sewing stores.

6. Egg-blowing tool Easter eggs that you intend to save must be blown out, and this tool makes the job easier. Gently pierce the egg at one end with the tool, then the other. Insert a piece of wire or other thin object into one end to break the yolk. Replace the tool at one end and squeeze the bulb to force the egg out the other side.

7. Bone folder This tool makes creases in paper and cardboard without cutting. Using a ruler as a guide, run the bone folder along the paper to make an indentation where you will be folding.

BAGS AND ENVELOPES

1. Glassine This milky-white, nearly transparent paper is resistant to moisture and oil. Traditionally an archivists' material, glassine lends itself to lots of other ideas. Used mostly by stamp collectors, these can hold gift cards (punch a hole and attach with ribbon or string) or a few cookies or candies as party favors. Use the paper itself as a second layer of wrapping over solid or patterned papers; it softens the appearance of whatever material lies beneath it.

2. Paper bags Brown-paper sacks are just the beginning of paper bags. They are also available in white and many colors. Decorate them as gift bags, use them as luminarias, or, of course, pack them with snacks and lunches.

3. Cellophane bags These clear, glossy bags have a festive shine and crackle. They are the perfect wrapping for cookies, pastries, and sweets. Or fill them with anything you choose. Decorate them for any occasion by tying them with ribbons and gift tags.

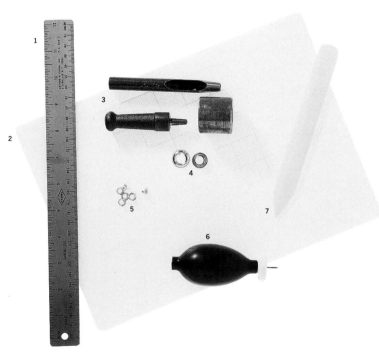

RIBBONS AND TIES

Ribbon has many personalities: A supple satin bow is elegant and opulent; polka-dot grosgrain is cheerful and sprightly; plush velvet is rich and luxurious. The sampling here only hints at the variety available. For the best selection, shop at good fabric and notions stores and specialty trimmings shops. Try looking in the yellow pages under "Ribbons." Remember that ribbons should always be recycled; save the ribbon on any present you receive. Iron it, and it will look fresh and new, ready to be wrapped around another gift and passed on to its next owner.

1. and 2. Organdy So sheer it's virtually transparent, organdy ribbon can be floppy or crisp, of a single color or shimmering and iridescent.

3. Rickrack Traditional trims, such as this rickrack, also make playful ribbons.

4. and 5. Satin The most fluid and dressy of all ribbons, satin is available in a vast range of colors and widths.

6. Fancy trim Once you start looking, you'll find ribbon and trim in stripes, dots, plaids, and countless varieties of fabrics, finishes, and patterns.

7. Seam binding This classic sewing notion comes in many colors and makes inexpensive, charming ribbon.

8. Waxed linen twine This thin, sturdy twine gives an informal, natural-looking finish; the wax makes it easy to tie into secure knots. Also very handy for tying on handmade gift tags.

9. Satin cord Thin and shiny, satin cord is particularly good for lacing and makes an elegant, colorful alternative to plain string or twine.

10. Grosgrain The crosswise ribs create a subtle elasticity and also give the ribbon a substantial, tailored appearance.

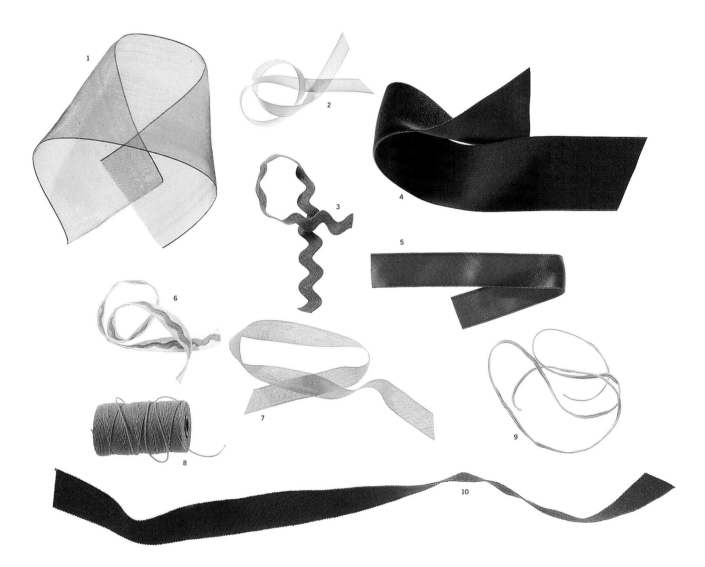

sewing basics

Needle and thread are two of the most versatile tools in the craft kit. Add a sewing machine and a few well-chosen accessories, and you're ready for almost any sewing project. Here are some basic techniques, each explained in detail, and tips for supplying your sewing basket.

SEWING A SEAM

Joining two pieces of fabric together in a perfect straight seam is essential for almost every sewing project.

With the right (front) sides of fabric together, pin fabric where the seam will be; pins should be perpendicular to the cut fabric edge as shown *(below left)*. The most common seam allowance called for is ⅝-inch; this refers to the distance between the edge of the fabric and the seam. On many machines, a marking on the throat plate helps you guide the fabric. With the presser foot raised, position the fabric so the needle is about ½ inch from the top edge. Lower presser foot and reverse stitch just to the top edge, then begin stitching forward; the reverse stitching keeps the seam from unraveling. Guide the fabric with your hands as you go.

Machines can generally stitch over needles, but it's not a bad idea to remove along the way. When you reach the end, reverse stitch again, about ½ inch. Raise the presser foot, gently pull fabric away, and clip the threads. Press seam open so the seam allowance lies flat against the fabric.

Seam finishes *(below center)* keep fabric from unraveling and make a seam more durable. Two easy finishes are shown here. For the one on the left, zigzag close to the edges, then trim as close to the zigzag stitching as possible. For the one on the right, Stitch about ¼ inch from the edges, then trim with pinking shears.

Finishing seams is essential in a garment like an unlined jacket, whose seams are visible and endure a lot of abrasion. For something like a pillow cover, whose seams go unseen, it may not be necessary, but it will help the cover hold up better and last longer.

After sewing a curved seam, clip small notches *(below right)* so the fabric lies flat when it's turned right side out.

SEWING KIT

It's easy to overstock a sewing basket, so instead of buying things you don't need, start with these essentials, and add specialty supplies as needed.

1. Fasteners Hooks and eyes and small snaps are easy to replace if they fall off.

2. Sewing-machine needles Match the needle to the fabric. General-purpose sharp-point needles are good for most woven fabrics. Use ballpoints for knits. Use finer needles with fine thread for fine fabric; thicker needles with thicker thread for thick fabric.

3. Buttons Keep on hand a small supply of plain buttons in various sizes.

4. Seam ripper This tool opens seams almost effortlessly. Use it with care to keep from ripping into the fabric.

5. Safety pins Store them this way so they don't become scattered in the basket.

6. Hand-sewing needles With a package of assorted-size needles, you'll be prepared to work on different fabrics; the same general rules apply as for machine needles. Needles called sharps are best for everyday stitching and mending; ballpoints should be used on knits.

7. Needle threader To use this handy tool, slip the flexible wire loop through the eye of a hand needle, feed thread through it, and pull the wire back out, bringing the thread with it.

8. Tailor's chalk Use a block of chalk to mark fabric before cutting or to guide you in making alterations.

9. Thimble Wear a thimble on your middle finger when hand sewing; use it to push needle through.

10. Beeswax A coating keeps thread from tangling when hand sewing; keep it in a plastic holder with slots to slide the needle and thread through.

11. Measuring tools Use a tape measure for measuring soft, curved things, and a yardstick for fabric on a work surface.

12. All-purpose thread All-purpose thread lives up to its name—it is appropriate for most hand and machine sewing. Use extra-thin thread on particularly fine fabrics; heavy-duty thread on very thick fabrics. Buttonhole twist is good for decorative stitching and sewing on buttons. Buy thread in the colors you wear most.

13. Pin holder A magnetic holder can be used to pick up scattered pins.

HAND STITCHES

Three hand stitches will get you through most basic tasks: the slip stitch, backstitch, and running stitch.

Thread a needle with a twenty-four-inch length of thread. Knot just one end; it's not necessary to sew with a double thickness of thread.

Use the slip stitch for hems. It is durable and virtually invisible—the thread is hidden inside the fold of the fabric, protected from wear and tear. The backstitch approximates the straight stitch on a sewing machine. It is strong, and perfect for mending a seam. The running stitch, called basting, joins pieces of fabric together temporarily. Novices may want to baste before sewing.

When sewing on a button, give it a thread shank (to create space between the fabric and button), allowing the button to slip through the buttonhole easily. This is essential on thick fabric, but it's useful for any button.

After hand stitching, the thread has to be tied off: Take a tiny stitch on the wrong (back) side of the fabric; before pulling the thread all the way through, send the needle through the loop of thread. Pull the thread until a second small loop forms, send the needle through that, then pull taut.

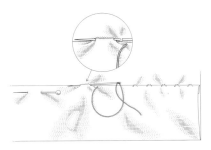

SLIP STITCH Make a small fold, just enough to encase the raw fabric edge; press. Then make another fold the size of the hem. Put the needle inside the fold, push it through to the front single layer of fabric, and pick up just a thread or two. Send the needle back into the fold. Repeat.

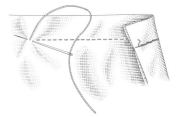

BACKSTITCH With right (front) sides of the fabric together, bring the needle through the two layers of fabric. Insert the needle back down through the fabric about $1/8$ inch to the right; bring it back up the same distance to the left of where you started. Repeat.

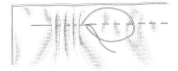

RUNNING STITCH Insert the needle at evenly spaced intervals into the fabric several times, then pull needle and thread through. Repeat.

SEWING ON A BUTTON Hold the button in place, and send needle from the back up through one of the holes. To create a thread shank, place a toothpick over the button *(left)*, then stitch down over it, into next hole. Stitch until each set of holes has been bound five or six times. With needle and thread between fabric and button, remove the toothpick. Lift up the button, and wrap the thread around the exposed threads between the button and fabric several times *(right)*. Tie off the thread under the button.

the guide

Items pictured but not listed are from private collections. Addresses and telephone numbers of sources may change prior to publication, as may price and availability of any item.

entertaining

page 13
Dremel Moto-Tool **drill,** *from Dremel, 4915 21st Street, Racine, WI 53406; 800-437-3635. Free catalog.* Four-ply **waxed linen twine,** $8.50 per spool, *from the Caning Shop, 926 Gilman Street, Berkeley, CA 94710; 510-527-5010. Free catalog.*

page 14
Quinces are available seasonally from: Dean & DeLuca, *560 Broadway, New York, NY 10012; 212-226-6800 or 800-221-7714.* Sid Wainer & Son Specialty Produce and Specialty Foods, *2301 Purchase Street, New Bedford, MA 02746; 508-999-6408 or 800-423-8333.*

pages 16 and 17
Cotton and linen **dish towels,** $4.50 to $23 each, *from Ad Hoc Softwares, 410 West Broadway, New York, NY 10012; 212-925-2652.* "Hon fleur" **plaid fabric,** $66 per yard, *from Pierre Deux, 870 Madison Avenue, New York, NY 10021; 212-570-9343.* "Cadenet" **plaid border,** *from Schumacher, 800-332-3384 for nearest retailer.*

page 20
2" custom **desk embosser,** $35 to $50, *from Empire Stamp & Seal, 36 East 29th Street, New York, NY 10016; 212-679-5370 or 800-998-7826.* Paper **napkins,** $1.99 to $4.75 per package, *from Village*

Paper, 18 Greenwich Avenue, New York, NY 10011; 212-675-9697.

pages 21 to 24
Sewing machine (#1260), $3,199, *from Bernina of America, Inc., 800-405-2739 for nearest retailer.* Cotton **pinpoint-oxford cloth,** $11.95 per yard; Kent Irish **handkerchief linen,** $24.95 per yard; **flax-tweed linen,** $29.95 per yard; and Swiss cotton **organdy,** $24.95 per yard, *from B&J Fabrics, 263 West 40th Street, New York, NY 10018; 212-354-8150.* Deka permanent **fabric paint,** $1.87 per ounce, *from Pearl Paint Co., 308 Canal Street, New York, NY 10013; 212-431-7932 or 800-221-6845.*

page 25
Yellow-striped **dish towel** (#67-641555), $12 for set of 4, *from Williams-Sonoma, 800-541-2233. Free catalog.*

page 27
Small **glassine envelopes,** $1.60 for 25, *from Apec, 900 Broadway, New York, NY 10003; 212-475-1204 or 800-221-9403.*

page 28
Bakelite **buttons,** $12 to $20 each, *from Tender Buttons, 143 East 62nd Street, New York, NY 10021; 212-758-7004 and 946 North Rush Street, Chicago, IL 60611; 312-337-7033.* Cotton **seersucker,** $9.95 per yard, *from B&J Fabrics, 263 West 40th Street, New York, NY 10018; 212-354-8150.* Assorted **buttons** are available from: Hersh Sixth Avenue Buttons, *1000 Sixth Avenue, New York, NY 10018; 212-391-6615.* K Trimming, *519 Broadway, New*

York, NY 10012; 212-431-8929. M&J Trimming, *1008 Sixth Avenue, New York, NY 10018; 212-391-9072.* Tender Buttons, *143 East 62nd Street, New York, NY 10021; 212-758-7004 and 946 North Rush Street, Chicago, IL 60611; 312-337-7033.* 1¼" white **elastic,** 80¢ per yard, *from Hersh Sixth Avenue Buttons, 1000 Sixth Avenue, New York, NY 10018; 212-391-6615.*

page 29
Linen-lined dough-proofing **baskets,** $35 to $40, *from French Baking Machines, 2666 Route 130, Cranbury, NJ 08512; 609-860-0577.* Natural **linen fabric,** $15 to $30 per yard, *from B&J Fabrics, 263 West 40th Street, New York, NY 10018; 212-354-8150.* #15 French **linen thread,** $8.50 per 50-gram spool, *from Talas, 213 West 35th Street, New York, NY 10001; 212-736-7744.* **Edible flowers,** $2.99 for 12, *from the Green House Fine Herbs, P.O. Box 231069, Encinitas, CA 92023-1069; 619-942-5371, ext. 118, for nearest retailer.* **Glass bowls** (#67-536060), $30 for 11-piece set, *from Williams-Sonoma, 800-541-2233. Free catalog.*

page 30
26-gauge **nickel silver,** $5.95 per 6"-by-12" sheet; **metal snips,** $12.60 to $22.75; **center punch,** $1.45 to $18.95; and 18-gauge **iron wire,** $6.75 per spool, *from Metalliferous, 34 West 46th Street, New York, NY 10032; 212-944-0909 or 888-944-0909. Catalog $4. (Minimum order $25.)* **Candles,** $20 to $32, *from Susan Schadt Designs, 348 South Cedros Avenue, Solana Beach, CA 92075; 619-793-0400 or 800-459-4595.* Small

fluted **tartlet pan**, $3.75 each; Goren Flot **hexagonal mold**, $29.90; and square **dough cutter**, $14.50 for set of 6, *all from Lamalle Kitchenware, 36 West 25th Street, New York, NY 10010; 212-242-0750. Catalog $3.*

cooking

page 35
Mustard seeds, $2 to $3 for 7 ounces, and **peppercorns,** $2.50 to $3 per ounce, *from Kalustyan's, 123 Lexington Avenue, New York, NY 10016; 212-685-3451.* 6-ounce **spice jars,** $1.25 each, *from Broadway Panhandler, 520 Broadway, New York, NY 10012; 212-966-3434.*

page 36
Mandoline, $29.50, *from Katagiri, 226 East 59th Street, New York, NY 10022; 212-838-5453.*

page 39
Ibarra Mexican **chocolate,** $5.25 for 12 ounces, *from Dean & DeLuca, 560 Broadway, New York, NY 10012; 212-226-6800 or 800-221-7714.*

page 40
Fini **balsamic vinegar,** $10.50 for 8.8 ounces, *from Williams-Sonoma, 800-541-2233. Free catalog.* Carandini **balsamic vinegar,** $55 per ¼ liter, *from Balducci's, 1102 12th Street, Long Island City, NY 11101; 800-225-3822.*

page 45
Kitchen **twine,** $5 per spool, and all-purpose **kitchen shears,** by Wüsthof, $18 each, *from Williams-Sonoma, 800-541-2233. Free catalog.*

celebrating

page 50
Heart **lollipop molds,** $8, and 3" to 6" **lollipop sticks,** $2 for 100, *from Sweet Celebrations, 800-328-6722. Free catalog.* 4" and 6" **lollipop sticks,** $2 for 100, *from New York Cake & Baking Distributor, 56 West 22nd Street, New York, NY 10010; 212-675-2253 or 800-942-2539. Catalog $3.* Small **cellophane bags,** *from Melissa Neufeld, Inc., 510-417-0750 for nearest retailer. To the trade only.* **Cellophane sheets,** *available at stationery stores nationwide.* ½"-wide

rayon **seam-binding tape,** *available at notions stores nationwide.*

page 51
25"-by-37" Japanese **Moriki paper,** $8.75 per sheet, *from Kate's Paperie, 561 Broadway, New York, NY 10012; 212-941-9816 or 800-809-9880 for free catalog.* Berol Prismacolor Blanc **white pencil** (PC 938), 85¢ each, *from A.I. Friedman, 44 West 18th Street, New York, NY 10011; 212-243-9000 or 800-736-5676.*

page 53
Copper **heart cookie-cutter set,** $45 for set of three (includes heart with fluted edge, hand with heart, and mini-heart cutters), *available from Martha By Mail, 800-950-7130.* 2" **heart cookie cutters,** 75¢ each, and **powdered egg whites,** $4.95 for 4-ounce bottle, *from Broadway Panhandler, 477 Broome Street, New York, NY 10013; 212-966-3434.* Powdered **food coloring,** $3 per vial, and **parchment paper,** $4 per 20' roll, *from New York Cake & Baking Distributor, 56 West 22nd Street, New York, NY 10010; 212-675-2253 or 800-942-2539. Catalog $3.*

page 55
Egg blower, $6.50, *from Surma, 11 East 7th Street, New York, NY 10003; 212-477-0729.* Assorted **ribbons** and **rickrack,** *available at fabric and notions stores nationwide.* Small **daisies,** $1.50 per dozen, *from Cinderella Flower Co., 60 West 38th Street, New York, NY 10018; 212-840-0644.*

page 56
½"-round Avery **labels;** 1¼" Times Bold **vinyl letters; paper burnisher,** $2.90 per dozen; and ¼"-wide 3M **masking tape,** $3.62 per roll, *from A.I. Freidman, 44 West 18th Street, New York, NY 10011; 212-243-9000 or 800-736-5676. Also available from art-, office-, and stationery-supply stores nationwide.* Silk **daisies,** $2 each; **silk ranunculuses,** $20 for 36; **antique roses,** $2 for 3; and **velvet leaves,** $2 each, *from Dulken & Derrick, 12 West 21st Street, New York, NY 10010; 212-929-3614.* Green **China silk,** $10 per yard, *from Felsen Fabrics, 264 West 40th Street, New York, NY 10018; 212-398-9010.* **Seam binding,** *available at notions stores nationwide.*

page 58
Mini **ball-peen hammer,** $2.25, *from*

Metalliferous, 34 West 46th Street, New York, NY 10036; 212-944-0909 or 888-944-0909. Catalog $4. (Minimum order $25.) 2" **wired ribbon,** $5 per yard, *from M&J Trimming, 1008 Sixth Avenue, New York, NY 10018; 212-391-9072.* ⅛" **hole punch** (#312-9559), $2.95, and **pastel paper bags** (#406-7229), $4.50 for 28, *from Sax Arts & Crafts catalog, P.O. Box 510710, New Berlin, WI 53151; 414-784-6880 or 800-558-6696.*

page 59
Crystallized flowers, *from Meadowsweets, R.D. 1, Box 371, Middleburgh, NY 12122; 518-827-6477.* Just Whites powdered **pasteurized egg whites,** $9.99 for two 8-ounce boxes, *by Deb-El Foods Corp., P.O. Box 876, Elizabeth, NJ 07206; 908-351-0330. Also available at supermarkets nationwide.*

page 61
7-piece Niji **wood-carving set** with sharpening stone, $6.19, *from Pearl Paint Co., 308 Canal Street, New York, NY 10013; 212-431-7932 or 800-221-6845.*

page 65
Almond paste, $5 for 7 ounces; **paste food coloring,** $1.25 to $1.99 per ounce; 9"-nonstick **rolling pin,** $10; metal **maple-leaf cutters,** $10 for set of 3; **leaf veiners,** $5 to $8 each; and **marzipan,** $5 for 7 ounces, *from New York Cake & Baking Distributor, 56 West 22nd Street, New York, NY 10010; 212-675-2253 or 800-942-2539.* **Mini-Bundtlett pan,** $20, *from Williams-Sonoma, 800-541-1262 for store locations.*

page 67
Silver-plated **candlestick,** $95, *from Claiborne Gallery, 452 West Broadway, New York, NY 10012; 212-475-3072.*

page 68
Knotted **cuff link,** $7.50 per pair, *from Barneys New York, Seventh Avenue at 17th Street, New York, NY 10011; 212-593-7800.* Vintage **postage stamps,** $10 for 4, *from Cambridge-Essex Stamp Co., 3998 Fifth Avenue, New York, NY 10016; 212-689-1142.*

page 69
Menorahs, *from Grand Sterling Company, Inc., 345 Grand Street, New York, NY 10002; 212-674-6450.* Honeycomb

beeswax, 87¢ to $1.25 per sheet, *from Rainbow Enterprises, 668 Turkey Hill Road, East Earl, PA 17519-9665; 717-445-6674.* Candle wicking, 15¢ per yard, and beeswax sheets, $7.95 for 10 sheets, *from Brushy Mountain Bee Farm, 610 Bethany Church Road, Moravian Falls, NC 28654; 800-233-7929.* Antique and vintage silver cups, $100 to $200 each, *from R&P Kassai, 1050 Second Avenue, New York, NY 10022; 212-838-7010.*

page 71
¾" dot stickers by Avery, $7.45 for 1,000, *from Staples Direct, 8 Technology Drive, Box 1020, Westboro, MA 01581; 800-333-3330.* Needle quilling tool, $2.50, *from Lake City Crafts, P.O. Box 2009, Nixa, MO 65714; 417-725-8444.* Gütermann silk thread, $1.75 per spool, *from Greenberg & Hammer, 24 West 57th Street, New York, NY 10019; 212-246-2467.*

giving

page 74
Silk taffetas in stripes and solids, $36 to $95 per yard, available from: ABC Carpet & Home, 888 Broadway, New York, NY 10003; 212-473-3000. B&J Fabrics, 263 West 40th Street, New York, NY 10018; 212-354-8150. Loose dry lavender, $2 per ounce, *from Terra Verde, 120 Wooster Street, New York, NY 10012; 212-925-4533.* Paperwhites, $3.75 for 5 bulbs, *from John Scheepers, 23 Tulip Drive, Bantam, CT 06750; 860-567-0838. Free catalog.* Indonesian river stones, $3.75 per pound, *from Smith & Hawken, 800-776-3336.* Green canvas cotton, $9.95 per yard, *from B&J Fabrics, 263 West 40th Street, New York, NY 10018; 212-354-8150.* 2" pink satin ribbon, $4 per yard, *from Hyman Hendler & Sons, 67 West 38th Street, New York, NY 10018; 212-840-8393.*

page 75
Small white daisy (#110), $1.50 per dozen; white daisy (#2070), $2.25 for six; and 3" hat pin, $3 per dozen, *from Cinderella, 60 West 38th Street, New York, NY 10018; 212-840-0644. (Minimum order $30.)*

page 76
Plastic flower vials, $14.95 for 100, *from*

Kervar, 119-121 West 28th Street, New York, NY 10001; 212-564-2525.* 4" to 6" grosgrain ribbons, $10 to $15 per yard, *from Hyman Hendler & Sons, 67 West 38th Street, New York, NY 10018; 212-840-8393.*

page 77
Pinking shears, $36.95, *from Steinlauf & Stoller, 239 West 39th Street, New York, NY 10018; 212-869-0321 or 800-637-1637.* Antique ribbons, *from Bell'occhio, 8 Brady Street, San Francisco, CA 94103; 415-864-4048.*

page 79
Essential oils, $11 to $24, *from Aveda, 800-328-0849 for nearest salon.* Stainless-steel canister, $12, *from Terra Verde, 120 Wooster Street New York, NY 10012; 212-925-4533.* 8-cup panadoro mold, $18.95; Cathedral pudding mold, $17.95; fluted mold, $17.95; and 6"-by-6" tinned-steel cake pan, $10, *from Bridge Kitchenware, 214 East 52nd Street, New York, NY 10022; 212-838-6746 or 800-274-3435.* Key-ring tags, $1.30 for 6, *from Reader's, 35 East 10th Street, New York, NY 10003; 212-473-8480.* 10" ceramic pie plate, $25, *from Williams-Sonoma; 800-541-2233. Free catalog.* White cup (DRPC003), $30, *from Wolfman-Gold & Good Company, 117 Mercer Street, New York, NY 10012; 212-431-1888.* Tea balls, $5 to $25 per box, *from G.H. Ford, 800-832-8068.*

page 81
Soap-making kit, $24 (includes 3 one-pound blocks of unscented glycerin soap, 3 bottles of coloring, and an assortment of reusable molds in rectangle, square, domed bar, round, and flower shapes), *available from Martha By Mail, 800-950-7130.* Unscented glycerin soap, *by Pure Pleasure; 800-856-0956 for nearest retailer.* Essential oils, $11 to $24 per ounce, *from Aveda. Call 800-328-0849 for nearest salon.* Melton wool, $29.95 per yard; rayon satin, $4.95 per yard; and silk-faced satin, $34.95 per yard, *from B&J Fabrics, 263 West 40th Street, New York, NY 10018; 212-354-8150.* Dardenelles brown wool/mohair yarn (#2276/50g), $6.95 per 95-yard skein, *from Classic Elite Yarns, 12 Perkins Street, Lowell, MA 01854; 508-453-2837.*

page 82
Rotary cutter (#315-1339), $13.60, and

scalloped blade (#314-1397), $8.55, *from Sax Arts & Crafts catalog, P.O. Box 510710, New Berlin, WI 53151; 414-784-6880 or 800-558-6696.*

page 83
French wooden beads, $1 each, *from Enchanted Forest, 85 Mercer Street, New York, NY 10012; 212-925-6677.* Handmade paper clips, $10 for heart and square set, $15 for 2-letter set, *made to order by Jodi Levine, 212-522-3255.* Custom tool sets, $24.95 to $61 (includes wire cutter, flat-nose pliers, round-nose pliers, and chain-nose pliers), and 20-gauge annealed-iron wire, $7.30 for 2-pound spool, *from Metalliferous, 34 West 46th Street, New York, NY 10036; 212-944-0909 or 888-944-0909. Catalog $4. (Minimum order $25.)* 1½"-by-3" custom rubber stamps, $15, *from Rubber Stamps, 30 West 24th Street, New York, NY 10010; 212-675-1180.* Color Box opaque-pigment stamp pads, $7 each, *from Kate's Paperie, 561 Broadway, New York, NY 10012; 212-941-9816 or 800-809-9880 for catalog.* Archival glue, $4.50 for 8 ounces; archival ink-spreading kit (#125), $15; and custom book-plates, *from Talas, 568 Broadway, New York, NY 10012; 212-219-0770.* White Strathmore crack-and-peel adhesive paper, $32 for box of 100 8½"-by-11" sheets, *from Namark Nobel Printing, 122 West 27th Street, New York, NY 10001; 212-463-8713.*

gardening

page 84
Birdhouse gourds, $18 to $42, *from Marder's, P.O. Box 1261, Bridgehampton, NY 11932; 516-537-3700.* Birdhouse- and ornamental gourd seeds, $1.50 per package, *from the Cook's Garden, P.O. Box 535, Londonderry, VT 05148; 802-824-3400.*

page 86
Ikebana shears (#7504), $35, *from Smith & Hawken, 800-776-3336.* Mundial 8" dressmaker's scissors, $21, *from Steinlauf & Stoller, 239 West 39th Street, New York, NY 10018; 212-869-0321 or 800-637-1637.* 2" peat pots, $1.95 for 30, *from Chelsea Garden, 205 Ninth Avenue, New York, NY 10011; 212-929-2477.*

page 89

Moss, *available at florists and garden centers nationwide.* Japanese **river stones,** $8.90 for a 2-pound bag, *from Grass Roots Garden, 131 Spring Street, New York, NY 10012; 212-226-2662.*

page 91

20-gauge dark **annealed iron wire,** $7.30 for 2-pound spool, and 100-mesh **brass screen,** $12 to $14 per square foot, *both from Metalliferous, 34 West 46th Street, New York, NY 10032; 212-944-0909 or 888-944-0909. Catalog $4. (Minimum order $25.)* **Hyacinth glasses** (#8871), $19 for set of 3 jars with 3 bulbs, *available from Smith & Hawken, 800-776-3336. Free catalog.*

page 92

Dried **hydrangeas,** $16 for a bunch of 6, *from Green Valley Growers, 10450 Cherry Ridge Road, Sebastopol, CA 95472; 707-823-5583.* Dried **hydrangeas,** $4 to $6 per head; 24" round **wreath forms,** $1.75 to $2.50; and green **floral wire,** $1.75 per ¼ pound, *from Joe Makrancy's Garden and Floral Shop, 966 Kuser Road, Trenton, NJ 08619; 609-587-2543.* **Hydrangea plants,** $18 to $35, *from Louisiana Nursery, 5853 Highway 182, Opelousas, LA 70570; 318-948-3696. Catalog $4.*

page 93

Deluxe **grow lamp,** $18, *from Home Depot, 800-553-3199 for store locations.*

decorating

page 96

36-gauge **aluminum foil,** $6.50 per 10' roll, and **metal snips,** $12.60 to $22.75, *from Metalliferous, 34 West 46th Street, New York, NY 10036; 212-944-0909 or 888-944-0909. Catalog $4. (Minimum order $25.)* **Ornamental nails,** $5 for 100, *from BZI Distributors, 105 Eldridge Street, New York, NY 10002; 212-966-6690.* 25"-by-38" **butcher's paper,** 48¢ per sheet, *from Pearl Paint Co., 308 Canal Street, New York, NY 10013; 212-431-7932 or 800-221-6845.*

page 97

Brass, copper, steel, aluminum, and bronze **wire mesh,** $7.50 to $17 per square foot, *from Metalliferous, 34 West*

46th Street, New York, NY 10036; 212-944-0909 or 888-944-0909. Catalog $4. (Minimum order $25.)

page 99

Circa-1920 American **medicine cabinet,** $350, *from Historical Materialism, 125 Crosby Street, New York, NY 10012; 212-431-3424.* **Clip-art books,** $3.95 to $11.95, *from Dover Publications, 31 East Second Street, Mineola, NY 11501; 516-294-7000.*

page 100

Bulldog **binder clips,** 99¢ to $1.19, *from Staples Direct, 8 Technology Drive, Box 1020, Westboro, MA 01581; 800-333-3330.* **Zinc molds,** $8 to $150, *from Urban Archaeology, 285 Lafayette Street, New York, NY 10012; 212-431-6969.* Vatican Art **casting stone,** $8.50 per box, and **SuperElasticlay,** $8.67 per pound, *from New York Central Art Supply Co., 62 Third Avenue, New York, NY 10003; 212-473-7705 or 800-950-6111. Free catalog.*

page 101

4" blue satin **ribbon,** $18.50 per yard, and society **double-faced satin,** from $7.50 to $15 per yard, *from Hyman Hendler & Sons, 67 West 38th Street, New York, NY 10018; 212-840-8393.*

page 103

Nineteenth-century clear-glass **oil lamps,** $28 to $85, *from Sage Street Antiques, corner of Route 114 and Sage Street, Sag Harbor, NY 11963; 516-725-4036.* 20" Urban **lampshade,** $45, *from Oriental Lamp Shade Co., 223 West 79th Street, New York, NY 10024; 212-873-0812.* ⅜"-**manila rope** and Weldbond **glue,** *available at hardware stores.*

page 104

7"-by-7" sconce **frame,** $39, *from Shades Lighting, 183 Bowery, New York, NY 10002; 212-388-1111. Free catalog.* 36" Dulkote **pressure-sensitive backing,** $58.30 for 10' roll, *from Service Fabrication Corp., 1935 Fairfield Avenue, Chicago, IL 60647; 815-356-6101.* Filmoplast T cloth **bookbinding tape,** *from Talas, 568 Broadway, New York, NY 10012; 212-219-0770. Catalog $5.*

page 106

Brass **café clips,** $5 each, *from Bed, Bath, and Beyond, 620 Sixth Avenue, New York, NY 10011; 212-255-3550 for other store locations.*

page 107

Handkerchief linen, $20 to $25 per yard; **heavyweight linen,** $20 to $30 per yard; and **pima cotton,** $6.95 per yard, *from B&J Fabrics, 263 West 40th Street, New York, NY 10018; 212-354-8150.* **Crochet lace,** $12 per yard, *from Inez MacWhinnie Antiques, Main Street, Bridgehampton, NY 11932; 516-537-7433.*

page 108

Linen, $15 to $30 per yard, *from B&J Fabrics, 263 West 40th Street, New York, NY 10018; 212-354-8150.* 2'-by-9' **foam,** $21.25 per sheet, *from BZI Distributors, 105 Eldridge Street, New York, NY 10002; 212-966-6690.* ½" **batting,** $11 per bag, and **cotton interfacing,** $3.50 per yard, *from Steinlauf & Stoller, 239 West 39th Street, New York, NY 10018; 212-869-0321 or 800-637-1637.*

page 109

Linen canvas, available from: New York Central Art Supply Co., *62 Third Avenue, New York, NY 10003; 212-473-7705.* Pearl Paint Co., *308 Canal Street, New York, NY 10013; 212-431-7932 or 800-221-6845 for catalog.* **Leather,** *available at leather stores nationwide.* **Tacks,** $5 for 100, *from BZI Distributors, 105 Eldridge Street, New York, NY 10002; 212-966-6690.*

page 111

Wooden **switch plate,** $3.68, *from Presley Crafts Manufacturing, P.O. Box 949, Rowlett, TX 75030; 800-886-2687.* Glass **switch plate,** $12, *from Rosen Paramount Glass, 45 East 20th Street, New York, NY 10003; 212-532-0820.* Galvanized-steel **buckets,** $25 to $30, *from William Wayne & Co., 845 and 850 Lexington Avenue, New York, NY 10021; 212-288-9243 or 800-318-3435.* Ronan Japan **matte enamel paint** and **lettering enamel,** $4 to $8.50 per 8-ounce can, *from New York Central Art Supply, 62 Third Avenue, New York, NY 10003; 212-473-7705.* Deka water-based **sign paint,** $6 to $12 for 8 ounces, *from Pearl Paint Co., 308 Canal Street, New York, NY 10013; 212-431-7932 or 800-221-6845 for catalog.*

homekeeping

page 114

Homosote board, *available at lumberyards nationwide.* 54" **linen** (#5653),

$24.87, from Pearl Paint Co., 308 Canal Street, New York, NY 10013; 212-431-7932 or 800-221-6845 for catalog. Assorted **ribbons** by C.M. Offray & Son are available at sewing stores nationwide. Assorted ribbons by the yard: 1½" to 6" **grosgrain**, $4 to $15; double-faced society **satin**, from $7.50 to $15; **moiré**, $2.80 to $20; **velvet**, $2.25 to $9; **plaid and dotted**, $1.30 to $15; **satin**, $1 to $4; **picot-edged**, $2 to $8.75; and **plaid taffeta**, $2 to $12.50, from Hyman Hendler and Sons, 67 West 38th Street, New York, NY 10018; 212-840-8393. **Antique ribbons** by the yard: **checkerboard moiré**, $26; ruffle-edged **grosgrain**, $3; **organdy**, $5.50 to $14; **plaid**, $12 to $15; **damask**, $12; and **pleated-satin**, $7.50, from Bell'occhio, 8 Brady Street, San Francisco, CA 94103; 415-864-4048. **Grommet kit**, $9, from Home Depot stores nationwide, call 800-553-3199 for store locations. **Copper gutters** available wherever roofing supplies are sold.

page 115
6" **bone folder**, $4.50, and 2½" **awl**, $2.25, from New York Central Art Supply, 62 Third Avenue, New York, NY 10003; 212-473-7705 or 800-950-6111. Free catalog. Waxed **linen thread**, $8.50 per 130-yard spool, from the Caning Shop, 926 Gilman Street, Berkeley, CA 94710; 510-527-5010.

page 116
Pavo **key cabinet**, $13, from IKEA, 412-747-0747 for East Coast locations and 818-912-1119 for West Coast locations. Woven **wicker drawers** (#201063254), $29, from Hold Everything, P.O. Box 7807, San Francisco, CA 94120-7807; 800-421-2264. 2¼"-3½" **coin envelopes** (#266866), $6.79 for 250, from Staples Direct, 8 Technology Drive, Box 1020, Westboro, MA 01581; 800-333-3330. Waxed **linen thread**, from the Caning Shop, 926 Gilman Street, Berkeley, CA 94710; 510-527-5010. Upholsterer's **stitching twine**, $7.95 per spool, from BZI Distributors, 105 Eldridge Street, New York, NY 10002; 212-966-6690. Ballpoint **hooks**, 38¢ to 90¢, from Simon's Hardware & Bath, 421 Third Avenue, New York, NY 10016; 212-532-9220. **Drawer pulls**, $5 per pair, from Garber Hardware, 49 Eighth Avenue, New York, NY 10014; 212-929-3030.

page 118
Sewing notions, from Greenberg & Hammer, 24 West 57th Street, New York, NY 10019; 212-586-6270 or 800-955-5135. Free catalog.

page 119
American Automobile Association (AAA), 800-564-6222 for membership information. Roadside and **accident assistance kits**, $25 to $45, from Premiere Safety Products, 800-842-7815.

page 120
Maine **garden tote**, $29, from L.L. Bean, 800-221-4221. Free catalog. 12" **drafting brush**, $5.60, from Pearl Paint Co., 308 Canal Street, New York, NY 10013; 212-431-7932 or 800-221-6845 for catalog. Spray **bottle**, $2.99, from Bed, Bath, and Beyond, 620 Sixth Avenue, New York, NY 10011; 212-255-3550. **Woven-grass boxes** (2½", 3½", and 4½" cube set and 11"-by-16½" rectangle), from Via Motif, 2915 Kerner Boulevard, Suite L, San Rafael, CA 94901. Write for nearest retailer. Canvas **makeup bags**, $6.95 to $12, from Ad Hoc Softwares, 410 West Broadway, New York, NY 10012; 212-925-2652.

page 121
Antique **linen toweling**, $25 to $45, from Paula Rubenstein, 65 Prince Street, New York, NY 10012; 212-966-8954. Dritz **eyelet kit**, $1.89, from Steinlauf & Stoller, 239 West 39th Street, New York, NY 10018; 212-869-0321 or 800-637-1637. Free catalog. ($30 minimum mail order.) 1" **linen tape**, $1.05 per yard, from New York Central Art Supply, 62 Third Avenue, New York, NY 10003; 212-473-7705 or 800-950-6111. Free catalog.

page 122
1½" Avery Clear View **binders**, $7.45 each; disk and document **sheet protectors**, $2.15 per 5-pack; laser **organizer pages**, $15 for 100 sheets; **self-laminating sheets**, $17 for 50; 4"-by-6" **laser postcards**, $18.49 for 100; and Rogers' **index-card box**, $2.65, from Staples Direct, 8 Technology Drive, P.O. Box 1020, Westboro, MA 10581; 800-333-3330. Free catalog. Labels from **clip-art books**, $3.95 to $11.95, from Dover Publications, 31 East Second Street, Mineola, NY 11501; 516-294-7000. **Binders**, $13.50 each, from Kate's Art Supply, 2 West 13th Street, New York, NY 10011; 212-675-6406. Bigso **document files** with ties, $13.50 each, from Sam Flax Art & Design, 425 Park Avenue, New York, NY 10022; 212-620-3060. 5"-by-7" Photoguard **photo sleeve** (#7719), $8 per package of 25, from Light Impressions, 439 Monroe Avenue, P.O. Box 940, Rochester, NY 14603; 800-828-6216. Custom **rubber stamps**, from Empire Stamp & Seal, 36 East 29th Street, New York, NY 10016; 212-679-5370.

page 124
Nature's Grip **rug hold pad**, $6.99, from Gracious Home, 1220 Third Avenue, New York, NY 10021; 212-517-6300. Colored plastic **spill-stop pourers**, $10 for 24, from the Everyday Gourmet, 2905 Old Canton Road, Jackson, MS 39216; 601-362-0723. Phoenixware **stopper with cap**, $2.79 per pair, from Lechter's Housewares stores nationwide.

page 125
Assorted **dish towels**, from Broadway Panhandler, 520 Broadway, New York, NY 10012; 212-966-3434.

page 126
Velvet, $14.95 to $100 per yard, available from: B&J Fabrics, 263 West 40th Street, New York, NY 10018; 212-354-8150. Rosen & Chadick, 246 West 40th Street, New York, NY 10018; 212-869-0136.

flower and leaf templates

Use for paper baskets on page 58. Trace onto paper, and cut out with a utility knife.

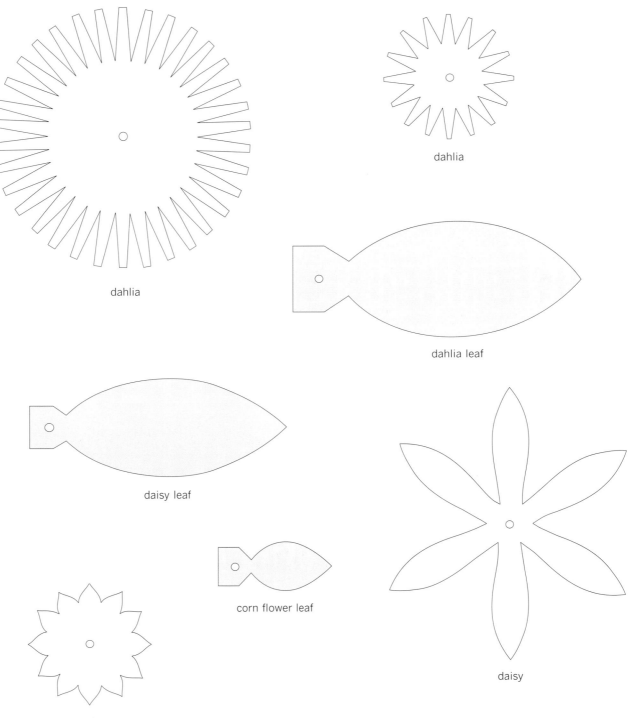

dahlia

dahlia

dahlia leaf

daisy leaf

corn flower leaf

corn flower

daisy

picture credits

photography

William Abranowicz front cover.

Melanie Acevedo pages 78 (top row: right), 121 (center), 126 (bottom).

Anthony Amos pages 2, 6 (top left), 26, 32, 34 (top left, center) 36 (right: top and middle), 38 (bottom row), 61 (bottom left and right), 82, 86 (top row: center), 125 (bottom right), back cover (middle left).

Fernando Bengoechea pages 29 (top left and center, bottom), 40 (bottom left, right).

Henry Bourne page 78 (bottom row: right).

Anita Calero pages 12 (top row; center row: left), 15, 80, 81 (top), 83 (top).

Reed Davis pages 20–25, 30 (bottom), 31, 34 (bottom), 38 (top left), 41, 42 (bottom right), 44 (top row: center and right; middle row; bottom row), 48, 50, 59, 77, 78 (top row: left and center; middle row: left and right; bottom row: left and center), 83 (center, bottom), 85, 86 (top row: left and right), 88 (bottom), 89 (left), 92, 97, 98, 100 (center, bottom row), 102, 103 (top row), 105, 106, 107 (top), 109, 112, 114 (top), 116 (top row: left and center; second row: right), 118, 120 (center), 124 (bottom left), 127 (bottom), 128–131, back cover (top left).

John Dugdale endpapers, pages 101 (top left), 114 (bottom).

Richard Felber page 88 (top).

Don Freeman page 9.

Dana Gallagher pages 6 (bottom), 28 (bottom left and center), 51, 55 (bottom left and right), 56 (bottom left and right), 62 (bottom), 76, 86 (center row), 93, 94, 96, 108, 111 (bottom), 116 (middle row: left; bottom row: center and right), 121 (top), 124 (top left), 127 (top), back cover (top right).

Gentl & Hyers pages 3, 6 (third row: right; fourth row), 12 (bottom row: right), 14 (top), 29 (top right), 30 (top left and right), 42 (top left), 44 (top left); 46 (middle row: center and right), 54, 55 (top row), 58, 60, 61 (top row), 89 (top right), 103 (bottom), 110, 116 (middle row: center), 120 (top), 122.

Thibault Jeanson pages 6 (top right), 16, 17, 18, 19 (top), 71 (top row: right; bottom), 111 (top).

Stephen Lewis pages 5, 10, 14 (bottom), 36 (left: top and center; bottom: left and right); 42 (top right), 43, 46 (top row; middle row: left), 62 (top), 68, 69 (bottom), 77, 81 (bottom), 86 (bottom row: center), 90, 91, 99, 101 (top right), 104, 107 (bottom), 114 (right), 115, 116 (top row: right), 120 (bottom), 121 (bottom), 125 (top, bottom left), 126 (top), back cover (middle center, bottom left).

Charles Masters pages 40 (top), 56 (right column), 57, 124 (bottom right).

James Merrell pages 6 (second row), 66, 67, 69 (top), 70, 72, 74.

Amy Neunsinger pages 132, 133.

Victoria Pearson pages 8, 28 (top left).

Grant Peterson pages 19 (bottom), 28 (right: top and bottom), 34 (top right), 75.

Victor Schrager pages 52, 71 (top row: left; middle row), 89 (bottom right), back cover (middle right).

Ann Stratton pages 38 (top right), 46 (bottom row), back cover (bottom right).

Jonelle Weaver pages 6 (third row: left), 12 (middle row: right; bottom row: left and middle), 27, 64, 86 (bottom row: right), 100 (top right), 119.

illustrations

Harry Bates pages 101, 133.

index

*If you have enjoyed this book,
please join us as a subscriber to*
MARTHA STEWART LIVING *magazine.
Call toll-free 800-999-6518.
The annual subscription rate
is $26 for 10 issues.*